KNIGHTS

KNIGHTS

Julek Heller

Text by Deirdre Headon

Additional illustrations by

Philip Argent, Chris Collingwood, Adam Heller,

Stephen Lavis, Robin Lawrie

ENCORE EDITIONS

London

This edition published 1989 by
Encore Editions Limited
6 Warren Mews, London W1P 5DJ

First published 1982

ISBN 0 947792 32 5

Computerset by MFK Graphic Systems
(Typesetting) Ltd. Saffron Walden, Essex, England.
Colour separations by Fotographics Ltd
Printed & bound in Hong Kong
by Regent Publishing Services Ltd.

ACKNOWLEDGEMENTS
Philip Argent, pages 10, 24, 42, 60, 74, 92, 108, 124, 138, 156, 173 and 176
Chris Collingwood, page 170
Adam Heller, pages 22, 70, 72, 84, 86, 103, 122 and 152
Stephen Lavis, pages 61, 63, 66 and 69
Robin Lawrie, pages 137, 155, 177, 180, 183 and 185

Of the many books which have provided source material for *Knights* the most valuable were:

Richard Barber, *The Knight and Chivalry* (Longmans, 1970)
Leon Gautier, *La Chevalerie* (Paris, 1897)
W. C. Meller, *A Knight's Life in Days of Chivalry* (London, 1924)
C. Mill, *History of Chivalry* (London, 1841)

CONTENTS

INTRODUCTION

Out of the Dark Ages of western Europe emerged marauding bands of horsemen whose fighting abilities, based on brute force, made them pre-eminent in society. These were the knights, and in many European languages today the word itself (*chevalier* in French, *Ritter* in German) means a mounted warrior. Throughout medieval Europe knights, bound by feudal oaths of allegiance to serve and fight for their king or overlord, united to form an exclusive international brotherhood.

The figure of the gallant and chivalrous knight, pledged to fight evil and injustice, is the most popular image of the knight today. The medieval knight did eventually begin to act with courtesy and civilized behaviour, but only towards members of his own class, and the brutal and savage warrior of earlier times was never far away.

A knight did not think it wrong to terrorize people of the lower orders, or to extort money from his retainers so that he could maintain his expensive lifestyle. Indeed, many knights were no more than ruthless bullies and their cruelty was often notorious. One English knight, Sir Bevis of Hampton, killed in his lifetime nearly seven hundred people. But knights were also a mass of contradictions. It is said that after the infamous tenth-century French knight, Raoul de Cambrai, had pillaged a convent, raping the nuns and burning them alive, he suddenly remembered that it was a feast day and fell to his knees in prayer.

INTRODUCTION

Whatever his ties of fealty to his overlord, the knight was very much his own master. If insulted he would wage private wars. He held sway with absolute authority in the countryside surrounding his castle. If he felt like it he might become a robber knight – lurking in the forests, from which he would emerge to attack and rob travellers before returning to the security of his castle. If he did not possess land he would be a knight errant, and wander through the heavily forested and sparsely populated medieval landscape making a living from his prowess as a fighter.

Although many knights were distinguished by their personal courage, courtesy and physical strength, a less attractive, and all too common, quality was their unshakable belief in their own superiority. Although a knight might wage war on his peer knight, he would respect him because of his equal social standing. Sometimes the ties of brotherhood were so great that in one tale a knight killed his two infant sons so that their blood might be used to cure the sickness of his brother-in-arms.

The knight's martial profession was also his pastime, and he liked nothing better than to show off his skill in arms in the tournament arena. Sometimes in the mêlée the fighting would extend beyond the tournament ground, spilling over into the surrounding countryside. Land would be carelessly devastated, with no thought for the hardship this would cause to the peasants who lived there.

Although many of their activities were not laudable, knights did possess an infectious exuberance and zest for life. Not great thinkers, knights were men of action whose emotions were always near the surface: they were at their most dangerous and prone to excess when they were bored. If there were no battles or tournaments to fight in, time hung heavy on the knight's hands. His preferred recreations would be to hunt, hawk or fish. He would certainly eat and drink heartily: one knight during a harsh winter drank his way through a whole wine cellar. He might play chess or backgammon. He might sing and dance. He would certainly flirt with ladies, and would think nothing of seducing his female serfs. Another recognized relaxation was to let blood: thinning the blood was thought to cool the temper of a hot-blooded knight. At times of little activity the most welcome visitor to the knight's castle was the wandering minstrel, who would tell wonderful stories – perhaps even a tale of a celebrated incident in his host's career, embellishing the exploits with each telling.

The world populated by such heroes as Lancelot, Galahad, Gawain and Gareth, with its many perils, monsters, fair ladies and mysterious phenomena was, in the knight's mind, his world too. The edges of reality were, for the knight, conveniently blurred, for he was, in his own estimation, quite capable of achieving glory such as theirs. It was not for nothing that William the Conqueror's minstrel rode into the Battle of Hastings singing the 'Song of Roland' to spur on the Norman knights.

When Constantine the High King of Britain was slain by Vortigern, his sons Ambrose and Uther made war on their father's slayer. The usurper was killed and Ambrosius became king but when he died Uther ascended the throne.

Uther's chief counsellor was the wizard Merlin, a man possessed of great magical powers: he could read men's destiny in the formation of the clouds; he could see into the future and cast powerful spells. Uther trusted Merlin in all things, and when one day Uther saw the shape of a winged dragon marked out in the sky Merlin told him this meant that one day Uther would have a son who would achieve greatness far surpassing that of his father. From that time Uther called himself Pendragon, meaning 'dragon's head'.

To encourage peace among his nobles, who had until recently been at war, Uther summoned everyone to a great feast at his court. Among those gathered was Gorloise, the Duke of Cornwall, and his beautiful wife Igraine. Uther immediately fell in love with this woman, and began sending her gifts daily. Soon she grew troubled at the attention the king was paying her. Igraine begged her husband: 'Let us leave the court, husband, for I fear the king's favour can bring us no good.'

By the next day the Duke of Cornwall, his wife and retinue had departed. When

Uther discovered their flight his rage knew no bounds. Blind to his all-consuming desire for Igraine, he interpreted the Duke's departure as treason. He gathered an army and besieged the Duke of Cornwall in the well-fortified castle of Tintagel, where Gorloise had sent his wife for safe keeping.

The days went by and Uther's infatuation for Igraine grew stronger.

'I can think of no one but Igraine. How can I ease this torment?' Uther asked Merlin. 'You are a magician. Tell me how I can win her.'

'I have the power to bring this about,' said Merlin, 'but there is a price to pay.'

'I don't care what it is,' said Uther. 'I must have her.'

Merlin explained how he could cast a spell whereby Uther would take on the appearance of the Duke, in which guise he might lie with Igraine.

'It is destined that I do this for you. But by doing so I must claim the child that is to be born of this union. Within an hour of his birth you must give him to me, and I will rear him in readiness for his great destiny.'

This Uther promised to do, and when evening fell Uther, in the shape of Gorloise, was admitted to Igraine's chamber. The child was conceived that night.

But at the very time that Uther was with Igraine, the Duke of Cornwall was making a surprise attack on the High King's forces, during which he was slain. When news of Gorloise's death was brought to Igraine she was deeply troubled. How could her husband have been with her when all reports said he was at that time dead? She kept these thoughts to herself.

Uther, now victorious, came to woo Igraine, and when the time of mourning had passed he asked Igraine to be his wife. But Igraine was an honest woman and when she found she was carrying a child which could not be her husband's she bravely told Uther what had happened on the night of her husband's death. Uther then told her of Merlin's magic, and she agreed to become his wife.

They were soon married and when the child, a boy, was born Uther took him from his mother. In secret he went to a castle gate and handed the child to the waiting Merlin. Merlin carried the baby down the steep cliff from Tintagel and took him to a distant castle. There he entrusted the child, now named Arthur, to the care of the good knight Sir Ector. Asking no questions as to whom this child was, he promised to bring him up with his own son Kay.

Uther and Igraine had no more children and when Uther died dark days fell upon the land, for there was no heir to succeed him. Everyone believed that Uther's child had died at birth, and now the nobles competed to become king.

During this time Arthur grew to young manhood in the safety of Sir Ector's castle. Merlin watched over him carefully, waiting for the moment when the rightful High King should claim his crown.

ARTHUR

When Kay was dubbed a knight, Arthur became his squire and went with Kay to his first tournament. However, in all the excitement Arthur forgot to bring Kay's sword to the tournament ground. Arthur then remembered seeing a sword which was strangely embedded in a large stone in a churchyard. Rather than return all the way to their lodgings he went to this place and effortlessly drew the sword from the stone. What he did not know was that this sword had been placed there many years before by a wise man who had foretold that it would remain embedded there until it was claimed by the true king.

A crowd of astonished knights quickly gathered to see who this boy was who had freed the sword, for in the past many of them had tried unsuccessfully to claim it. Now it was the time for Merlin to reveal who the youth was. He drew back Arthur's sleeve and there, plain for all to see, was the mark of a dragon on Arthur's arm. This mark proved Arthur was indeed the son of the last king, Uther Pendragon, the son thought by most people to have died in infancy.

Many proud kings and knights, not surprisingly, scorned the right of this apparently low-born youth to be king. Instead they declared war against him.

Arthur's foremost adversary was the great warrior King Pellinore. When this king brutally killed one of his loyal knights Arthur determined to avenge the death. The impetuous young king rode out to meet and challenge King Pellinore. But Arthur was an inexperienced fighter and soon fell, badly wounded, beneath King Pellinore's mighty sword strokes. As Arthur lay stricken, his sword broken, King Pellinore moved in to kill the upstart king.

Meanwhile, however, Merlin had been watching the combat from a hiding-place, and seeing that Arthur was about to be killed he cast King Pellinore into a deep sleep. As Pellinore's great bulk sank heavily to the ground in charmed sleep, Merlin came forward to comfort Arthur.

The magician's glittering grey eyes were, for once, dimmed with sorrow, and with concern for the welfare of the young king. But he knew he had not the power to heal him. And so, helping the wounded youth to his horse, he mounted his own and the two men rode slowly away into an enormous forest to seek a hermit who, Merlin hoped, would heal Arthur's wounds.

They found the hermit in his small stone house, bent over a fire and watching a boiling pot. Great bubbles broke slowly on the surface of the liquid inside, and the air was filled with the aroma of herbs. As the hermit added more berries and twigs and leaves, the steam would rise and change colour. He turned to see who entered his dwelling and did not seem surprised to see Merlin.

'The birds told me that an old enchanter and a wounded knight were coming towards me, and I thought it must be you, Merlin. Who is the youth? Put him down to rest, for I see he is gravely wounded.' Arthur was laid down on a pallet of straw, where he closed his eyes and looked for all the world like a dead man.

Merlin crossed the floor to the hermit. They looked at each other, both knowing that Merlin had a favour to ask.

'This is Arthur, the noble son of Uther Pendragon. It is not time that he should die. His life has long to run, but unless you give him aid all the glories which his life holds will be lost. Even though I am a powerful magician, it is not in my power to heal him. That is why I am asking you. In three days we must continue our journey, for we must reach the lands of Avalon. There we will meet the Lady of the Lake, who has a special gift for Arthur.'

'I see you love this young king,' said the hermit, 'and it is my fortune to possess the skill to heal him.' The hermit immediately set to work administering healing balms to Arthur's wounds.

For two days and nights Arthur lay delirious in the cave, tossing and turning feverishly. Then as the medicines worked their way through his body, a change came over him. On the third morning he awoke refreshed, his wounds all but healed.

'Arthur, you must get up,' said Merlin, seeing him awake. 'Today we have a long way to travel.'

From the insistence in his voice Arthur knew it was no time to argue. Gingerly rising to his feet, he stumbled towards the door. He looked round to thank the hermit but his benefactor was nowhere to be seen.

Outside the hermitage the air was chill. Shivering, Arthur wrapped his cloak closer around him. Merlin gave a low whistle, at which their horses came forward from among the trees. The two men mounted, Merlin whispered in the ears of the horses, and with an answering whinny they cantered forward.

The horses seemed to know exactly where they were going. As they made their way through the tall trees, through thick undergrowth, across narrow streams and up mossy banks, they never faltered. Their speed caused a considerable breeze, and as they galloped Arthur seemed to hear the words 'Arthur is coming, Arthur is coming'. He felt he was being watched, and at times he could see the glitter of many pairs of eyes through the trees. Sometimes the branches of the trees looked like waving arms pointing the way forward. He rode in a state of wonder without asking what it all meant, or where this journey was leading them. But Merlin was silent.

At length they emerged from the forest and Arthur saw nestled beneath him between soft green hills a calm and very blue lake. At the far end of the lake he could make out the misty shapes of a chain of islands rising out of the water. Through a break in the distant hills he could see a massive plain reaching far out to the horizon.

'Oh, Merlin, where are we?' asked Arthur. 'If I had died I would have thought this were paradise, for this place makes me feel so at peace.' He sat up in his saddle and drank in the sweet air of the land.

'This is Avalon,' said Merlin. 'Note it well, Arthur, for you will never see it in such a light again. Beneath this lake and on those distant islands is the great kingdom of the Lady of the Lake.'

Their journey was now nearing its end and as they rode down towards the water Arthur felt that the moment of some great revelation was at hand. He reached the lake, dismounted from his horse and quickly made his way to the water's edge.

'I must drink,' he thought. Stooping down, he cupped his hands and dipped them into the lake. His fingers tingled as he raised the cold water in his cupped hands to his mouth. It was the purest, freshest water he had ever tasted.

Suddenly, he felt as if the sun was blazing straight on to his head and, as he looked up, he saw rising out of the centre of the lake a pale arm swathed in glistening white

samite. In its hand, held aloft and dazzlingly bright, was a mighty sword. The blade shone like the sun and from the jewels on the hilt blazed all the colours of the rainbow. It was so bright that Arthur had to turn his eyes away. Arthur knew that he must have this sword.

Merlin touched his arm and, reading his thoughts, said, 'It is your sword, Arthur. When you were born the swordsmiths in Avalon began forging this sword for the time when you should come to claim it. Through all the world they sought the finest jewels for the hilt and mined deep in the earth to find the purest gold in which to engrave its name: Excalibur. It is held in trust for you by the Lady of the Lake and you must ask her for it.'

As Merlin spoke the figure of a beautiful woman rose from the water, dressed in robes as blue as the lake itself. As she made her way across the water, gliding as smoothly as a swan, Arthur stood spellbound.

'Welcome, noble Arthur,' said the Lady. 'You have finally come for your sword. It is yours, but in return for it you must swear to grant me a gift whenever I ask for it.'

Anxious only to possess the sword Arthur took this oath without thinking. Then the Lady led him to a part of the shore where a small boat was concealed among the reeds.

'Go and claim your sword,' she said, and with these words she vanished.

Arthur stepped into the boat. It moved off from the shore as if rowed by invisible oarsmen, yet there was no sight nor sound of oars breaking water. The boat found its own course towards the centre of the lake, and soon the sword was within Arthur's reach. Leaning out of the boat Arthur took hold of the sword, at which the pale arm disappeared beneath the water. He gripped the sword. Its hilt fitted his hand perfectly. The handle seemed to be fashioned of gold leaves which furled round the handle like a vine round an olive tree. Armed with such a sword, Arthur felt he was a true king.

As he gazed on the sword, the boat returned him to the shore where Merlin was waiting for him. Arthur leapt ashore but would not let go of Excalibur. He held it aloft marvelling at the pure bright steel of the blade, which was tapered to a perfect point.

'Merlin, tell me, why does it bear the words "*Take me*" on one side and "*Cast me aside*" on the other?' the excited Arthur asked.

'Don't concern yourself,' replied Merlin, gently smiling at Arthur's delighted expression, 'but remember that plain beyond this lake and those hills, for that is where you shall fight your final battle. When that time comes you will have to return Excalibur to this lake.'

Although Arthur heard these words, he gave them hardly a moment's thought.

His only concern was for his sword – the glorious Excalibur. At that moment the Lady of the Lake appeared again. In her arms she carried a gold scabbard studded with jewels. It was attached to a belt made of the purest silk, into which dragons, the device of Arthur's father Uther Pendragon, had been woven with fine gold thread.

'Arthur,' said the Lady of the Lake, smiling, 'you like your sword well. But take this scabbard, too, for it is worth ten such swords. As long as you wear it you shall never lose blood through wounds in battle.' And so saying the Lady tenderly fastened the belt round Arthur's waist so that the scabbard hung on his left side. Then she disappeared.

It was now time for Arthur and Merlin to leave the land of Avalon. Arthur sheathed his precious sword and, mounting their horses, the two men set off for the kingdom of Logres. Arthur was now ready to fulfil his great destiny to found the noblest order of chivalry – the Knights of the Round Table.

THE SWORDSMITH'S WORKSHOP

The mystery and legend surrounding the forging of such magical swords as Excalibur were made more potent by the real-life secrecy maintained by the craftsmen who made the blade.

There was a healthy rivalry as to which countries made the best swords. Some knights held that Spanish swords made in Toledo were far superior to those made in Germany, where the feuding Hanseatic nobles ensured that the swordsmiths were never short of work, while others thought that the French swords made of Poitiers steel were the best. But it was a buyers' market, and a knight often bought a blade forged in one country and took it to another to have the hilt fitted.

Working in a hot and steamy workshop, the swordsmith smelted ores over charcoal to form a molten mass of steel. Once tested, this was taken to the anvil and hammered into a rough bar. Cutting pieces from this, the artisan layered them together, welding and drawing the pieces out to form the blade. In between each successive layering the emerging blade was tempered in water to make it strong and bright. The smiths of the famous sword-making centre at Saragossa boasted that their swords were the strongest and most brilliant owing to the waters of the river Ebro which flowed by the workshops.

The swordsmith could feel the quality of the blade he had made. If he found it too hard he would expose it to the open air to rust and become more flexible. He could also sense any weakness in the blade and would bury the weak part in charcoal powder on his forge's hearth to strengthen it.

The swordsmith knew that on his craftsmanship often depended not only the life of its owner but perhaps the destiny of a kingdom.

THE SWORD

The sword was the mark of the knight, one of his most prized possessions and a symbol of his high social and military standing. If, for some grave misdemeanour, a knight was stripped of his knighthood, his sword would be broken before his eyes. A sword, however, should not break. They were made to last a lifetime and often a sword was passed down from father to son, and each generation would add some design or jewel to the sword to make it his own.

When the bladesmith was satisfied that he had done his job, the newly-forged blade was given to the hafter, who made the handles. These craftsmen were responsible for the hilts, made of precious metals and often decorated with jewels. A knight would sometimes commission the hafter to incorporate some jewel or relic he had acquired into the hilt. These swords, by the nature of the materials used, often became ceremonial swords, which were not put to such rough use as the sword with the perishable grip.

Its cruciform shape, formed by the crosshilt or 'quillons', a transverse bar at the base of the hilt, also served as a potent religious symbol: in battle a fatally wounded knight would lift his sword before his eyes so that his last earthly sight would be the sign of the cross. Knights also incorporated relics into their swords, put religious inscriptions on the blade and often had their seals (for making their mark – few could write) incorporated. Relics were often set in the pommel. Knights somehow managed to find teeth, hair, blood, toenails and threads from garments that had belonged to various long-dead saints. Indeed, if all the teeth allegedly belonging to St Peter and found inside pommels were added together the poor man must have had at least ten full sets of teeth.

A sword was not complete without its scabbard. The most common scabbard, made by the sheather, was a wooden frame over which leather was stretched. More ceremonial swords had scabbards made of precious metals intricately designed and studded with jewels.

The sword was used for slashing rather than thrusting, and its shape changed little from the tenth to the fifteenth century. Its two-edged blade was 32-33 inches long and 2 inches wide, tapering to a point. Such a blade weighed about 2 lbs. The blade had to be razor-sharp, capable of severing a thread floating in the air. Godfrey of Bouillon on the First Crusade was reputed to be able to cut off a camel's head with a single slash of his sword.

Swords were sometimes imbued with mythic significance. Richard the Lionheart on his way to the Third Crusade gave to Tancred of Sicily, a sword which was believed to be the legendary Excalibur.

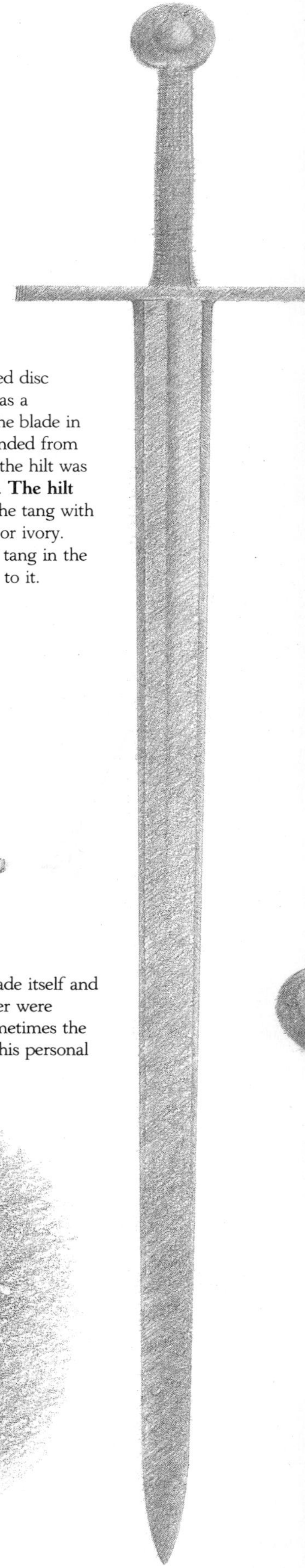

The pommel was a walnut-shaped disc attached to the tang which acted as a counterbalance to the weight of the blade in the knight's hand. **The tang** extended from the widest part of the blade, and the hilt was attached to this narrow extension. **The hilt** was often made by surrounding the tang with some hard material such as bone or ivory. This was either placed round the tang in the form of a sandwich or welded on to it.

Inscriptions were cut into the blade itself and thin wires of gold, silver or pewter were hammered into the incisions. Sometimes the engraver could not resist leaving his personal mark on the blade.

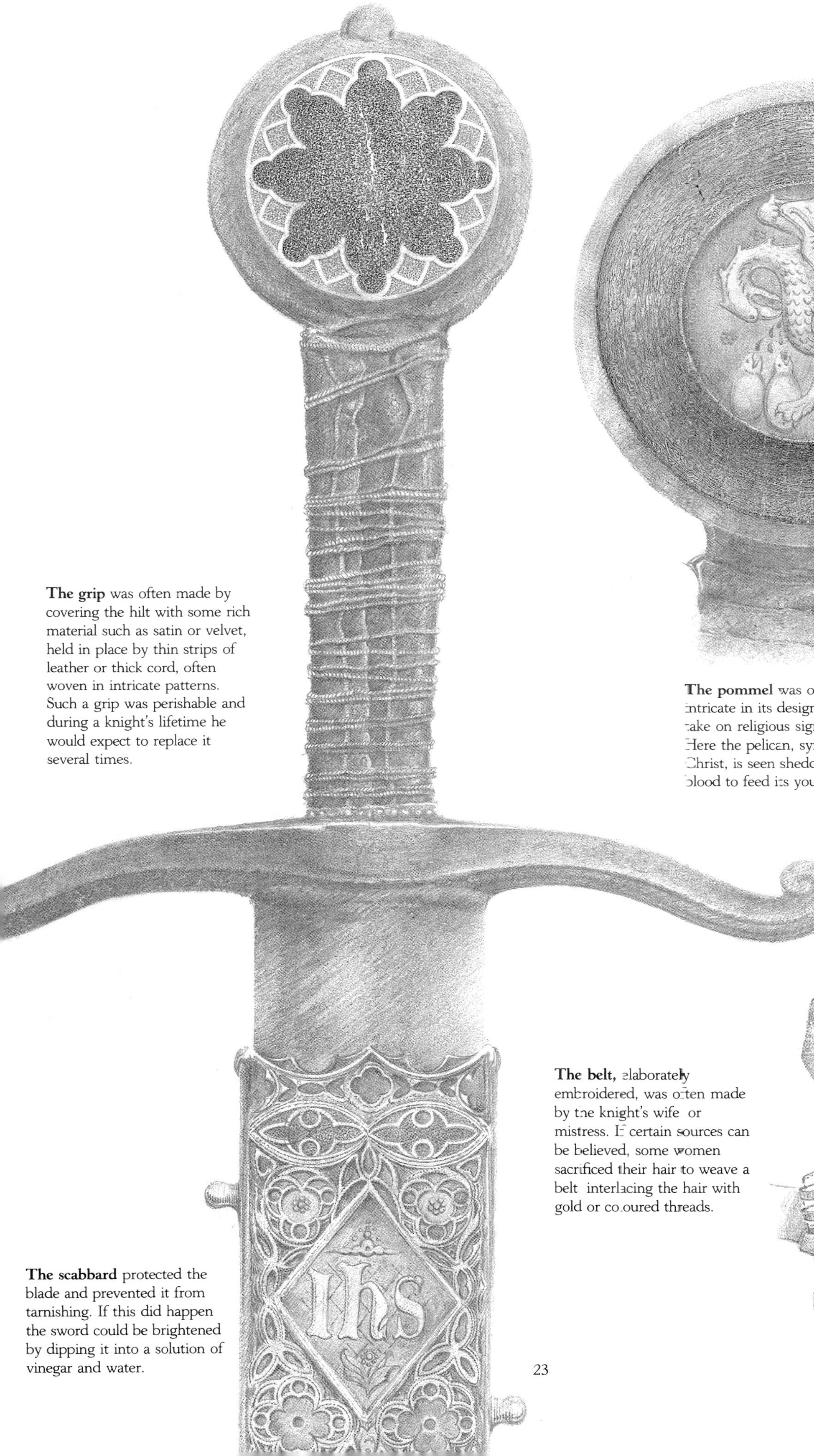

The grip was often made by covering the hilt with some rich material such as satin or velvet, held in place by thin strips of leather or thick cord, often woven in intricate patterns. Such a grip was perishable and during a knight's lifetime he would expect to replace it several times.

The pommel was often intricate in its design and could take on religious significance. Here the pelican, symbolizing Christ, is seen shedding its blood to feed its young.

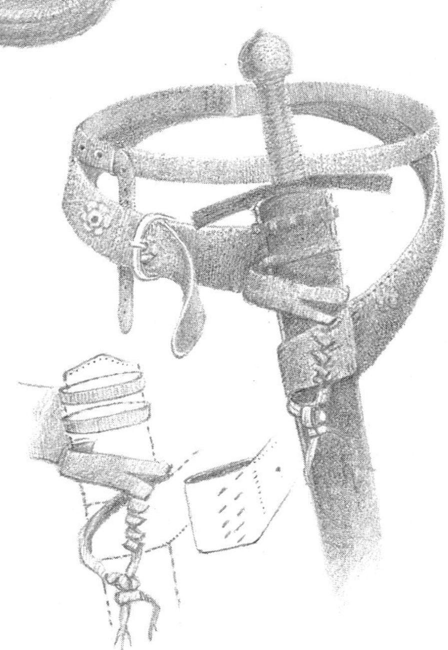

The belt, elaborately embroidered, was often made by the knight's wife or mistress. If certain sources can be believed, some women sacrificed their hair to weave a belt interlacing the hair with gold or coloured threads.

The scabbard protected the blade and prevented it from tarnishing. If this did happen the sword could be brightened by dipping it into a solution of vinegar and water.

SIEGFRIED

Siegfried was born without fear. As he grew so did his strength, boldness and skill in arms. In wielding a sword, casting a spear and riding a steed he outstripped all his companions. And when he was not increasing his physical prowess his tutor Regin taught him to play chess cunningly and to speak many languages. But Regin did not teach the boy from any good motive. He was an evil man – some people thought he was a sorcerer – and when he saw that Siegfried was so strong and brave, and completely lacking in cowardice, he knew that he had found a warrior capable of slaying the mighty dragon Fafnir. Regin planned that when Fafnir was dead he would become the owner of the dragon's fabulous treasure.

As Siegfried's skills increased Regin grew impatient. But Siegfried had a sunny nature and was quite happy to stay at the castle where he had grown up. Regin plagued him with questions in the hope of making him wish to go out into the world and find adventure.

'It is strange that though you are the best rider you do not possess a horse,' said Regin one day.

'Why?' asked Siegfried, shaking his curly head. 'Why should I want one when all I have to do is go to the stables and ask for one, and it is given to me?'

'If that is so,' replied Regin, 'ask the king if he will give you a horse of your own.'

So Siegfried went to the king and asked him. The king was delighted to grant this gift. Siegfried then asked Regin to help him choose his horse. However, when Regin went into the stables he started to act like a madman, setting free all the horses from their stalls. Wildly, his flowing robes fluttering and his arms waving like an old crow that cannot take flight, Regin drove the horses down to the fast-flowing river near the castle. Still Regin urged the horses on until, like lemmings, they all rushed into the torrent and were soon struggling against the current to regain the riverbank.

'Which horse shall be yours, Siegfried?' screamed the manic Regin.

Above the roaring water and the wild neighings of the horses Siegfried shouted: 'Why, the one that swims against the water, for he is stronger than all the rest.'

Siegfried immediately plunged into the foaming water and swam through the swell to the horse. Soon he had reached him and, throwing his arms around the horse's strong neck, he hauled himself on to its back. The horse liked the feel of his new rider and obediently swam back to the bank.

'My horse has the strength and the courage of a host of common beasts. He shall be with me all my life and carry me through all adventures. And I shall call him Grani.' Regin's face grew bright with evil pleasure, for Siegfried would soon be ready to undertake the quest to seek and slay the dragon Fafnir.

'You are still no warrior,' chided Regin, 'for although you have a horse you do not have a sword.'

'Then,' joked Siegfried, 'you shall make me one.' This Regin did. He went to the forge, heated the furnace and smelted the ore. From this he drew the blade and with mighty blows he fashioned a fine and sharp blade. When he had tempered it in water the sword shone bright. He attached the blade to a hilt and handed the newly-forged sword to Siegfried. Well-pleased, the youth swished the blade through the air and brought it down on the anvil to test its strength. But on contact the blade shattered into a hundred pieces.

'This sword is no good for me. Make me another,' said Siegfried, disappointed.

All day and all night Regin beat out blade after blade, the hammer blows falling fast and furious, but always the same thing happened. The forge's floor became littered with broken bits of metal.

Siegfried told his mother how he could not find a sword strong enough for him to wield. She went to a chest and drew out an object wrapped in a yellowing cloth. When the cloth was removed, a mighty sword was revealed, but its blade was in two pieces.

'This was your father's sword,' said his mother. 'When he was killed in battle his sword, Gram, broke in two. Take it and forge it afresh, for your father's sword should now be yours.'

Siegfried carried the broken sword to the forge. As he had seen Regin do, he stoked the furnace until it flamed red. Then he heated the broken metal. As he watched its colour turn from silver to red to white, the two broken pieces ran together, and the blade was made whole once again. Then he brought the blade down on the anvil. This time the blade did not shatter – but the anvil split in two.

That same evening Regin told Siegfried of his plan to slay the dragon Fafnir. Thinking of the glory such a conquest would bring him, Siegfried straight away

made ready to leave and seek out Fafnir. Not a word that he had heard of the monster's strength and savagery made Siegfried afraid.

The pupil and his tutor set out next day. As they rode through thick forests Regin cowered at the shadows cast by the great trees, and started at the strange, rustling sounds and ominous cracklings of the undergrowth. But Siegfried was unmoved by these terrors. At night the howling of the wolves did not disturb him, and even the gruesome grunts of the wild boars failed so much as to cause a hair to bristle on this fearless youth's neck.

Eventually their journey took them close by Fafnir's lair. Here the land was barren because the vegetation had been withered by the dragon's poisonous breath. Siegfried and Regin saw the tracks of the beast – giant footprints and, behind them, deep grooves where its great tail had dragged along the ground. Siegfried dismounted his horse and went to look at the tracks on the ground. Regin, however, remained firmly in the saddle. Suddenly the ground began to shake and the air was filled with the stench of sulphur. Fafnir was approaching.

Regin now grew even more frightened. He wanted to run away, leaving Siegfried to meet and fight the dragon. He turned his horse and was about to flee to the safety of some trees nearby when Siegfried called up to him.

'How can I kill it?' he asked.

Regin told him quickly what to do: 'Follow the dragon's tracks close to that yellow water' (the dragon's malodorous breath had turned it that colour). 'Dig yourself a pit near the bank and hide there. When the dragon comes to bathe he will crawl over your hiding place and you can strike him with a blow from beneath.'

'But might I not drown in the blood and water?' enquired Siegfried. There was no answer: Regin had already turned tail and run away.

Siegfried did as Regin suggested and when the great red body of Fafnir crawled over the hole where Siegfried lay hidden, he plunged his sword into the dragon's body right up to the hilt. Immediately Siegfried was covered in a flood of hot, black blood which mixed with the water which had rushed into the hole. Siegfried thought he would suffocate and he rose gasping to the surface. Where the dragon had fallen there was, luckily, just enough space for him to squeeze through into the open air. Fafnir was mortally wounded. As the blood flowed from his body he feebly raised his great horned head to look for his assailant.

His fast-dimming green eyes saw Siegfried: 'Beware the man who told you how to strike me,' said the dragon, 'for now he will slay you.' His monstrous head splashed into the water and Fafnir was dead.

Siegfried was exhausted. As he drew his hand across his face to wipe away his sweat a drop of the dragon's blood touched his lips. Suddenly, he could hear voices. Looking around, he found he could understand the speech of two birds perched on a bare tree nearby. He listened to them enraptured. The first bird was saying: 'If only Siegfried would drink the dragon's blood he would gain great wisdom.'

'Even if he did that,' replied the second bird, 'would he have enough wisdom to know that he should not trust Regin? Regin is planning to kill Siegfried, because all he wants is Fafnir's treasure. Siegfried should kill Regin first.'

'Yes, he should kill Regin,' echoed the first bird. 'And if only he would seek out the sleeping warrior maiden Brunhilde, she would teach him all the wisdom he lacks.'

As Siegfried heard these warnings he also remembered what Fafnir had said, so that when the gleeful Regin returned and saw the dragon dead, Siegfried did not give him time to draw breath but drew his sword and struck off his head.

Then Siegfried swiftly mounted his horse and followed the dragon's tracks, which led to Fafnir's lair. There he found a great storehouse of treasure – gold, jewels and all manner of precious ornaments – more than any mortal could ever desire. Siegfried piled many chests-full on to Grani's back, for the horse could carry ten times more than the strongest packhorse. But one particular piece caught Siegfried's

eye. It was a great gold ring. Siegfried picked it up and placed it on his finger. Then, laden down with gold and jewels, Siegfried left this place and went to seek the warrior maiden Brunhilde.

He rode for many miles, all the time keeping to the path that the birds of the air told him to follow. After several weeks he found himself at the foot of a great range of mountains, where his ears were filled with the booming sound of a roaring fire. As he gazed up he saw one peak glowing with a mass of flames which seemed to leap up to the heavens. Siegfried rode as near to this peak as he could and then left his faithful horse to continue on foot. Up the steep and stony mountainside he climbed, each step drawing him nearer to the fire, until he arrived at what proved to be a solid wall of flames forming a great circle. In the centre he glimpsed the sleeping figure of a warrior covered by a shield. The fearless Siegfried plunged through the flames, the fire causing him no harm at all. Inside the circle the ground was soft and mossy green. He approached the sleeper and lifted the shield. Then he touched the helmet and was surprised to see two flaxen braids of hair tumble free: the sleeping figure was a woman.

At his touch she stirred and opened her eyes.

'Who is the hero who ventures through the flames and breaks my sleep?'

'I am Siegfried, the slayer of Fafnir,' the hero replied. And knowing that this woman must be Brunhilde, of whom the birds had spoken, he asked her to teach him her wisdom.

Brunhilde willingly did this: through many long days, within the magic circle of fire, she taught him all that a warrior should know to make him victorious, and how, as a victor, he should rule.

By now, Siegfried and Brunhilde had grown to love each other, and they each swore never to love anyone else. At length, however, Brunhilde told Siegfried that it was not fated that they should live together for all time: instead, he would return to the world of men so that they might profit from the wisdom she had taught him. She also told him that there was great power in the ring that he had taken from Fafnir's lair and that he should give it to no man. Siegfried promised that one day he would return to Brunhilde. As he departed she kissed him for the last time and gave him magic powers so that, should the need ever arise, he would have the power to change his shape with that of other men.

Siegfried once again passed through the circle of flames and climbed down the mountainside to where Grani had been waiting for him all this time, laden with Fafnir's treasure. Rich beyond most men's wildest dreams, Siegfried returned to the world he had left what seemed like years before.

After many long days of travel he came to a great castle overlooking a city. Here he sought out a craftsman and, using some of Fafnir's treasure, he commanded the craftsman to make him a suit of armour from it. Night and day the craftsman worked, delighting in his task. The gold was so malleable that he created a suit of armour, bearing a splendid dragon device, that fitted Siegfried like a second skin. Yet the armour was not too heavy and Siegfried could move easily when wearing it. The faithful Grani was also duly equipped with armour emblazoned with the dragon symbol.

Now Siegfried went up to the castle. As he approached the king came out to meet this splendid knight, for all the inhabitants had cried out that a god was approaching. The king asked him who he was. 'I am Siegfried, the slayer of Fafnir,' replied Siegfried. 'You are welcome here,' said the king. 'All that I have is yours.'

Siegfried stayed long at this castle. Soon the people grew to love him for his unfailing courtesy and wisdom. They could trust his advice on any matter. His prowess as a warrior grew too, and he did great services for the king. Such was Siegfried's influence that the king's enemies were persuaded to become his allies.

Siegfried's companion-in-arms throughout this period was the king's son Gunnar. A gentle man, Gunnar had grown to love the fearless knight and would have laid down his life for him, even though Siegfried surpassed him in every feat, mental or physical.

The king also had a daughter, called Gudrun. As the months passed the queen,

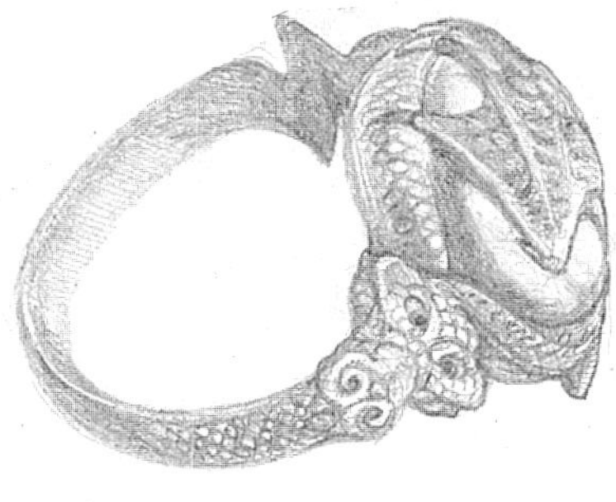

Grimhilde, noted how her daughter's eyes grew tender whenever she looked upon Siegfried. The queen thought how good a match Siegfried would be for her daughter. If they were wed then Siegfried would stay in this land, ensuring peace; what was more, he seemed to possess riches beyond measure. But first the queen questioned Siegfried to find out if he was promised to any woman. She discovered that Siegfried loved and had promised himself to Brunhilde.

But Siegfried's love of Brunhilde was no impediment to this queen, who was determined to procure him for her daughter. One evening she brought a goblet to Siegfried as he sat at table. The drink was laced with a potion that would make a man forget all his past life.

'Siegfried, your coming here has given us great joy. We wish you health and happiness. Drink this cup of friendship,' urged the queen.

Siegfried took the goblet gladly and drank. Immediately all his former life and his love for Brunhilde vanished from his mind.

The queen was anxious to see how the potion worked: 'Siegfried,' she asked, 'tell us once again the tale of the maiden who dwelt within the circle of flames.'

Siegfried shook his head, which suddenly felt heavy and for an instant his sight seemed dimmed.

'Madam, of what do you speak?' enquired Siegfried. 'I swear I do not know any such tale.'

Queen Grimhilde was now sure that her magic potion had done its work.

Siegfried and Gudrun were married amidst great rejoicing and they lived in great happiness. The marriage drew Siegfried and Gunnar closer together. They swore friendship and became blood-brothers. And indeed it seemed to many as if they might have been born of the same mother. Through the succeeding years they travelled through many lands making many conquests and increasing the power of the king.

But Queen Grimhilde did not rest. Gunnar was still unmarried, and Grimhilde now decided that there was only one woman worthy to be her son's wife: Brunhilde. No sooner had the queen told her son of her wish than the forgetful Siegfried gaily said that he would go with Gunnar and help him all he could to woo this woman.

All the while since Siegfried had left her, Brunhilde had been waiting on her mountaintop surveying the land beneath for the first sight of his return. Often she would gaze out and think sadly of the time they had spent together. But she would brighten when she thought to herself that Siegfried must one day return – for had he not pledged himself to her?

Then one day she saw two figures riding across the plain. Straining her eyes to make them out, she realized, with a pounding heart, that one of the horsemen was Siegfried. Soon the two men had reached the mountain and were clambering up its side. But when they drew nearer to the circle of flames Gunnar shrank back. Twice he steeled himself to plunge through the flames as Siegfried had told he would have to do. Both times his fear held him back. Ashen-faced, Gunnar had to admit that he was defeated by the flames.

'Don't fret, brother,' said Siegfried. 'For some reason beyond my knowledge I have the power to change my shape with other men. I shall change myself to look, and talk, like you and then go to woo Brunhilde, for the flames hold no fears for me. Brunhilde will never know the difference.'

Siegfried's shape was changed and he walked once again through the flames. But he failed to notice that throughout the transformation the dragon's ring remained on his fingers. Brunhilde rose joyfully and ran to meet the man with arms outstretched, for she believed it could be none other than Siegfried. Surely never in all eternity could a hero such as he be born again. But as she reached him she drew back: it was not Siegfried. Brunhilde's heart sank and her face grew pale.

'Who are you who have crossed the flames?' she asked in a trembling voice.

'I am Gunnar,' replied the transformed Siegfried. 'I have come through these flames to claim you as my wife.'

'That cannot be, for I am Siegfried's promised wife,' cried Brunhilde in despair. But the wretched Brunhilde knew that she was fated to marry the man who claimed her by crossing the flames.

'Siegfried is already wed,' said the man who called himself Gunnar.

'You lie,' sobbed Brunhilde. 'He would never forsake me!'

'Truly, Siegfried is married to my sister Gudrun.'

At these words Brunhilde drew back in despair. And then she saw the golden ring. She could not believe that Siegfried had given it away. She stood as if paralysed, her beautiful face overcast with grief. Her mouth grew hard and her eyes lost their lustre: so it was true – Siegfried had forgotten her.

At length she said: 'I consent to your wishes, Gunnar, for I vowed that I would marry the man who came to me through the fire.'

Then Siegfried ran back to Gunnar and, clasping him by the shoulders, told him of his success. Swiftly the two men regained their true shape.

Now Brunhilde crossed through the wall of flames to her betrothed. Immediately she saw that Gunnar's companion was her Siegfried. But he looked at her and did not know her. Brunhilde's anger mounted, and her heart turned to stone. Without a word she mounted Gunnar's horse to ride behind him.

When they returned to the castle everyone rejoiced to see Gunnar's beautiful

bride. They were soon married, and as they sat at the wedding feast Brunhilde looked on Siegfried and his fair wife Gudrun. Brunhilde's proud spirit came alive again within her hardened heart. Siegfried's insulting behaviour towards her had turned her great love to hate, and she vowed vengeance on Siegfried.

The wives of the two warriors spent much time together. One day Brunhilde saw Gudrun wearing the golden ring which Siegfried had worn.

'Who gave you that ring?' Brunhilde asked.

'Why, my husband Siegfried gave it to me,' replied Gudrun.

Suddenly it dawned on Brunhilde that the man who had come to claim her in Gunnar's shape had been none other than Siegfried.

The shock was overwhelming. From that moment she would neither eat nor drink, and as the days passed she grew steadily weaker. Gunnar became concerned, and asked his wife what ailed her. Then Brunhilde accused him of not being the man who had crossed the flames to win her. Gunnar's look of shame was all the evidence that Brunhilde needed to know that it was true.

Her single thought was that Siegfried should die. Day after day, growing weaker all the time, she begged and pleaded with Gunnar: 'Slay Siegfried – or I shall die!'

Gunnar's happiness was now destroyed, for he loved both his wife and his blood-brother. In desperation he sought his mother's advice. The queen blamed Siegfried for all this sorrow. She told Gunnar that Siegfried had once loved Brunhilde and that it was her magic potion which had made him forget her.

Gunnar was struck dumb, for now he saw clearly that his wife's sickness must have come from the love that she too felt for Siegfried. Then he remembered how Siegfried had often spoken of Brunhilde when he had first arrived at this land. Gunnar wondered how he could have forgotten such a thing, for he could not have sought the hand of Brunhilde if he had known that Siegfried loved her.

The queen said that she would set things to rights. But Gunnar had lost all trust in her, seeing her for the first time for the evil woman she was. Indeed this wicked queen's only trait of goodness was her love for her children. Now she decided that only Siegfried's death could resolve the situation; but so malicious was this woman that she was determined that Siegfried should not die until he had remembered all his past life.

That evening the queen presented a cup of wine to Siegfried in which she had mixed a magic philtre to restore his memory.

'Drink this, brave Siegfried, and tell us of your adventures before you came to our land,' said the queen.

Siegfried drank and without thought told of his exploits. He told of how he came by his sword, and how he slayed the frightful dragon Fafnir. And then he told of the flames through which he passed to find the warrior maiden Brunhilde. Then all the memories of that great love poured back into his mind and he rose in anguish.

'Brunhilde, how could I forget you? Why did I not return to you? My beloved . . .'

As he stood paralyzed with agony one of Queen Grimhilde's henchmen, who had been secretly instructed beforehand, stabbed Siegfried in the back and he fell dying to the floor.

Instantly uproar broke out in the castle. Disturbed by the noise, Brunhilde rose from her bed and entered the hall to see her Siegfried lying bleeding on the floor. All her hatred melted away, and she rushed towards him. As she cradled his head in her arms, Brunhilde felt that they were once more as one – as they had been when she had first shared her wisdom with Siegfried. For the last time she bent to press her lips on his. Even as she kissed him she felt his lips grow cold and his spirit slip away.

In her grief, the brave Brunhilde commanded a funeral pyre to be built, and there Siegfried was laid dressed in his gold armour with his sword clasped between his hands. Brunhilde was nowhere to be seen. Then, as the first torch lit the pyre, she appeared in her warrior maiden's clothing and mounted on Siegfried's horse Grani.

As the flames soared higher she cried out loud, 'My beloved, I come to join you!' and rode fearlessly into the fire. The pyre burned brightly, filling the sky with great red and blue flames. But, strange to tell, not a wisp of smoke rose from them, and when the fire was done there was no trace or mark upon the ground to show what a sorrowful occurrence had taken place there.

THE PAGE

Knights believed that the first morsel of food that a baby boy ate should be from the tip of his father's sword. It was hoped that having tasted the steel of the blade the baby would grow up into a brave knight, ready to lose his life with honour on the battlefield. However, it was at the age of seven that the future knight began his real training: he became a page.

Removed from his mother's care and women's company, the young boy was sent to the castle of an overlord or a relative. The castle was the only logical place for a boy to learn all the required knightly skills. Here there would be an armoury where he could find out about armour and weapons and a mews where he could learn to tend falcons; he would also meet the lady of the castle, from whom he would receive his first lessons in courtesy. She would expect him to run messages, too, and perform general household tasks.

The main part of the page's training took place in the tiltyard, an open meadow near the castle. Here he would take strenuous daily exercise – running, wrestling, learning how to wield a lance, spear and sword. He would be taught how to slash and parry strokes using a blunted sword. He would also, of course, learn to ride, and how to vault on to a bareback horse. Pages quickly became so skilled and developed such a good sense of balance that they could stand upright on the horse's back while it cantered. The emphasis on physical training meant that there was little time for formal education. In general, knights considered it more important for their sons to know how to blow a hunting horn and ride elegantly than to be able to read and write. These skills, it was felt, could be left to priests and clerks, for a knight counted for nothing if he was not a good warrior.

Pages, like all small boys, often quarrelled with their fellows; feuds started between boys in childhood sometimes continued into adult life. In England Fulk Fitzwarren, a page at the court of Henry II, quarrelled violently with the king's young son Prince John. In the end Fitzwarren kicked the young prince in the chest. For years Prince John harboured a grudge against him and when he became king he confiscated all Fitzwarren's lands. Fitzwarren responded by taking to the forests, where he attacked all the king's men who came his way.

The most tedious part of being a page was being used as an errand boy, but knights believed that if a boy was to become a good knight he had to learn to serve. Pages found it difficult, sometimes, to remember how to behave properly in the presence of their betters. *The Babees Book* (1475) contained useful reminders: a page should not sit until bidden; when spoken to he should not fidget, wriggle, scratch or lean against a post; and he should speak only when spoken to.

The time spent hunting, riding and falconing compensated in some degree for all these restrictions, but above all, the page could see within the castle the position and privileges enjoyed by knights and remind himself that one day he, too, would join their number.

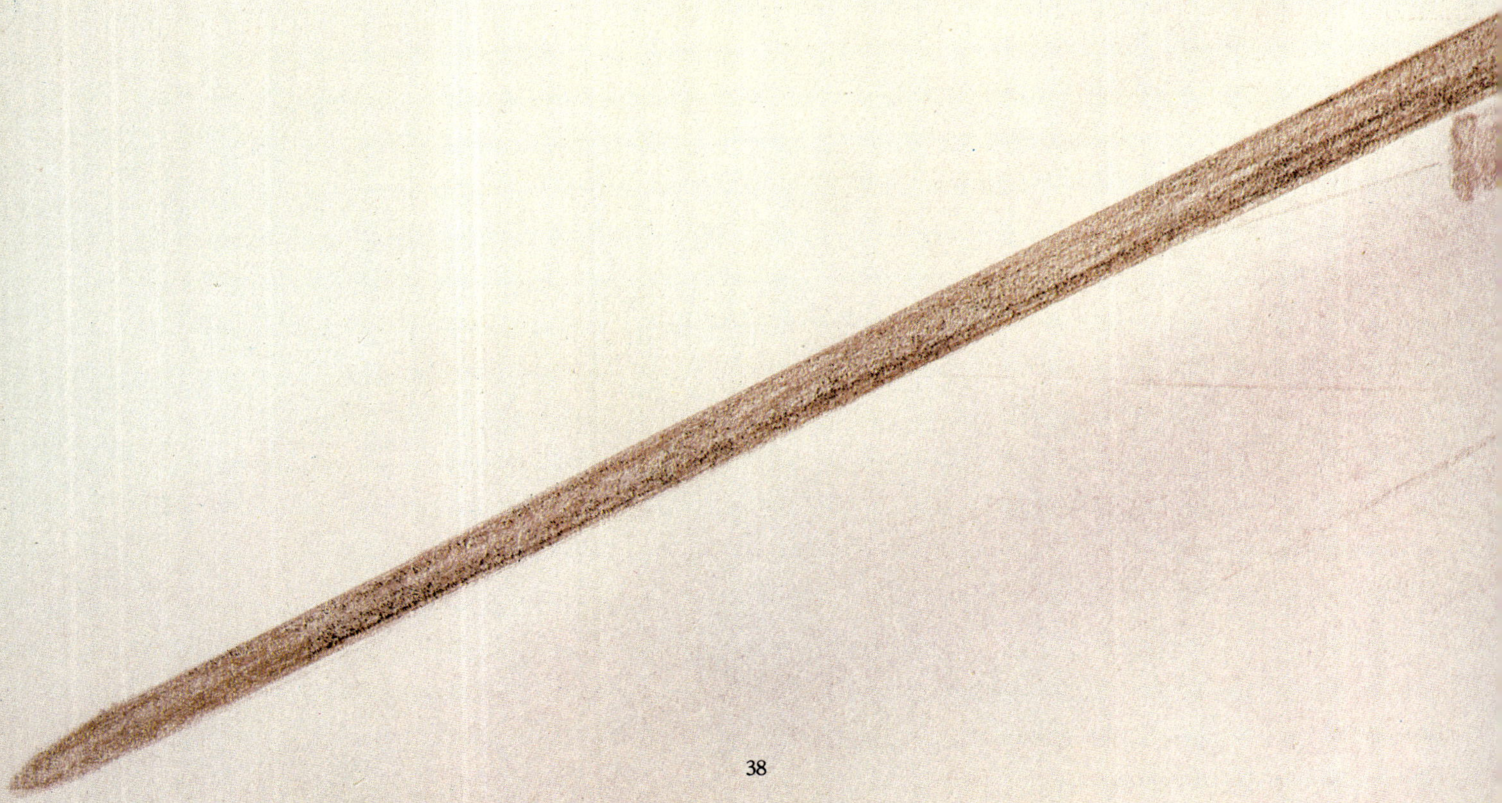

THE SQUIRE

The page became a squire at the age of fourteen. This occasion was sometimes marked with a simple ceremony in which the squire's parents, carrying lighted tapers, presented their son to the priest. He was then blessed and handed the sword and baldric of the squire.

The squire strove to perfect the basic skills learnt as a page. A favourite exercise was playing at the 'quintain', a large post of willow around which old hauberks covered with shields were fixed. Sometimes the quintain was brightly painted with the effigy of some well-known villain or infidel.

Sitting well back in the saddle, the squire galloped at the quintain holding his lance in his right hand, the base of it resting on the opposite side of his body to the target. He galloped at full tilt, aiming to hit the dummy squarely with his lance, using only his leg muscles to keep him on his horse at the moment of impact. If the blow was accurate he could break the quintain on impact. However, the quintain was designed to spin around at great speed if he made a false hit, so to avoid being knocked off his horse he had to duck quickly as he sped past.

For most of the time the squire was attached in service to a knight and would accompany him wherever he went, riding behind him on a horse called a roncin. Squires particularly enjoyed going to tournaments, for the day before the tournament proper all the squires were allowed to show off their skills by taking part in a mock tourney. During the tournament each squire stood in the lists ready to aid his knight, handing him a new lance when needed, or, if he were wounded, helping him from the field. Squires also guarded any prisoners taken and entertained the captives until a ransom had been agreed, taking pride on these occasions in showing how chivalrously they could behave.

However, after one tournament the squires were soundly reprimanded because a group of them, armed with sacks, had sneaked on to the tournament ground and pilfered any bits of armour or trappings they could find. Usually without any form of income, most squires were quick to seize on any chance to make money.

Whenever a knight went to war his squire rode with him, but it was a strict rule that squires should not take part in the battle. However, in the heat of battle it was inevitable that the occasional blow would be struck by a squire at the enemy, and he was, after all, permitted to aid his knight if he was in mortal danger.

The squire's whole life was governed by the notion of personal service to his knight. He would wake him up in the morning and help him dress. He would welcome visitors on his behalf. He would carve meat at the table according to special custom: a duck had to be broken, a hen despoiled and a peacock disfigured. His last duty of the day would be to help his knight prepare for bed. He then slept on the floor by his knight's bed in case his master should want him during the night.

It was believed that only by experiencing such training at first hand would a squire fully appreciate the honour and responsibilities of knighthood.

When he reached the age of twenty-one money had to be found to equip him for his initiation. This was a costly procedure and some squires from poor families never gathered the necessary resources. These men often remained squires, in service, for the rest of their lives.

When the noble knight Gahmuret was killed in battle, his wife Herzelöyde, who was expecting their child, vowed that the baby she was carrying would never learn what it meant to be a knight. Her husband's knightly endeavours had, after all, brought her nothing but sorrow. When her son was born she named him Parzifal, meaning 'pierced to the heart'.

True to her vow, Herzelöyde made sure that Parzifal grew up knowing nothing of knighthood, and all her serfs were ordered, on pain of death, never to talk to the boy about being a knight. Indeed, so far did she carry her desire that nothing should vex her son that when he wept tears of joy to hear the birds sing Herzelöyde ordered her servants to wring the necks of as many birds as they could catch.

Parzifal was a beautiful child who grew into a tall, straight and strong youth with the clear, large eyes of a falcon. Golden hair framed his noble features. Dressed in clothes made of animal skins, his greatest sport was to wander through the forest near his home hunting wild beasts and slaying them with crude bows and arrows he had made himself.

One day as Parzifal was out hunting deer in the forest he suddenly felt the ground shake beneath him with the sound of hoof-beats. Expecting to catch some large animal, he hid behind a thick shrub so that he could surprise his prey. Through the trees, at a gallop, rode four glorious knights mounted on magnificent chargers.

Parzifal was struck dumb. Never had he seen such a wonderful sight. The horsemen's armour glistened, and their horses' trappings glowed with bright colour. Parzifal was convinced that the foremost, and most lavishly dressed, of these men must be the god of whom his mother had told him.

Parzifal ran forward and lay down in the path of the horses. The riders reined in and looked down in wonder at this poorly-dressed youth. Despite his clothes, there was nobility evident in the boy's face.

Parzifal got up. As his curiosity overcame his feeling of awe, he began to examine the knights' armour. How, he wondered, were the links in the mail put together so tightly? (The only rings he had ever seen were those his mother's maids strung on ribbons.) 'Indeed,' he thought, 'if the animals I hunted had such a hard skin as this, not one of my arrows would pierce it.'

The chief knight of the four, Parzifal discovered, was a prince in pursuit of two wicked knights who had kidnapped a damsel. He asked the boy if he had seen the knights pass this way.

'What is a knight?' asked Parzifal. Astonished and yet amused at this fair youth's ignorance, the prince explained. He unsheathed his sword and told Parzifal that this was the weapon of a knight. He handed down his shield and let Parzifal hold it. He described what a knight did and Parzifal, his father's brave blood stirring in his veins, cried, 'I must be a knight. Who can make me one?'

'We are knights of Arthur of Britain's Round Table. If you prove yourself worthy he will make you a knight,' said the prince, and with that the knights galloped off, and were soon lost among the forest trees.

That evening Parzifal had a strange tale to tell his mother. As she listened she wept bitterly for now she realized nothing could prevent her son from leaving her to become a knight. She clothed him in rough woollen garments, fitted leather buskins to his legs and gave him a broken-winded horse to ride, secretly hoping that if Parzifal was much ridiculed he would quickly return to her. Then she gave him some

advice which Parzifal was to remember well. She told him to greet all men and women courteously. If possible, he should gain a woman's ring and, if the occasion arose, waste no time in kissing her. Her last instruction was that if an old, grey-haired man offered to teach him good manners Parzifal should accept.

Bright and early the next morning Parzifal set off. The people he met as he travelled could not but smile at the incongruous sight of this happy youth dressed and mounted so strangely and bidding them good day so politely.

Soon he came to a lush green meadow in which was pitched a many-coloured silken pavilion. Never before had Parzifal seen such a sight. He trotted across the meadow to the pavilion and got down from his horse. As he drew back the opening and ventured inside the pavilion his eyes opened wide in wonder at the marvellous sight before him. There, asleep on a richly draped couch, lay a beautiful woman. On her left hand Parzifal saw a ring which sparkled with bright stones. Remembering his mother's words he set about taking it for his own. As he struggled to remove it the woman awoke. Terrified to see this strange young man in her tent, she begged him to let her be. Then Parzifal remembered his mother's other lesson and he kissed the distraught woman. Now even more terrified, the woman gave Parzifal her ring, and the simpleton left, well-pleased with his prize.

He continued his journey and from the people he greeted, as his mother had instructed him, he learnt that he was not far from the place where he should find King Arthur. As he drew nearer he met a fearsome-looking knight clad in a magnificent red and gold suit of armour. In his hand was a golden goblet.

'Is this the way to King Arthur's court?' enquired Parzifal.

'Yes,' replied the knight, 'and if you are going there, tell Arthur that I, Ither of Gaheviez, shall wait here until he sends a challenger to try to take back this goblet which I took from King Arthur.'

Parzifal soon arrived at the court and delivered the message to King Arthur.

'Let me fight this Red Knight,' said Parzifal. 'I have learnt that a knight must wear armour. Since I have none, let me win this knight's armour so I, too, can be a knight.'

King Arthur was astonished at these words but he was still so angry at the Red Knight who had stolen the goblet from him even as he drank from it that, with hardly a second thought, he agreed to Parzifal's request.

Delighted, Parzifal rode across the courtyard and as he did so a peal of laughter rang out from a balcony from where Queen Guinevere and her ladies were watching the goings-on below. As Parzifal looked up he grew angry to see a knight slapping the face of the woman who had laughed. This was Lady Cunneware, who had vowed never to laugh until the best of knights rode before her. The knight who had struck her was Sir Kay, always an irascible man, who was disgusted to see that the

man who had at last made this lady laugh looked so very different from the accepted ideal of what a knight should be.

As he rode by Parzifal called up to the lady: 'Fear not, lady. I shall avenge you of the knight who struck you for my sake.'

Parzifal soon reached the meadow where the Red Knight waited for a challenger.

'Give me the goblet you stole from King Arthur,' said Parzifal. 'Yield to me and give me your armour.'

At this challenge the Red Knight exploded with rage: 'Insolent boy,' he roared, 'who taught you such strange manners? You will have to slay me if you want the goblet and my armour.'

Levelling his spear he charged at Parzifal confidently expecting to transfix his challenger with a single blow. But Parzifal, who was skilled in avoiding the charges of wild beasts, ducked and leapt nimbly from his horse.

The Red Knight roughly reined in his horse and wheeled around to charge again. As he thundered towards Parzifal the youth took careful aim and cast his spear. It whistled through the air and found its mark in the knight's neck just above the rim of his armour. The Red Knight fell backwards off his horse, dead.

The coveted armour was now Parzifal's. He tried to remove it and as he struggled, not knowing where to begin, a grey-haired knight rode up and showed him what to do.

The grey-haired knight had taken kindly to the youth, and told him of the misfortunes life had dealt him: 'I have lost three sons, in war and on great quests. Come to my castle and be my fourth son and I shall instruct you in all the ways of knighthood, for I see that there is much that you should learn to become a worthy knight.'

Parzifal went gladly with this gentle knight, Prince Gurnemanz, who, true to his word, instructed Parzifal in all the knightly arts: the use of arms, how to ride and how to defend himself. He also taught him how every knight should live, helping the weak and punishing the cruel and evil. Parzifal remained a long while at Prince Gurnemanz's castle but eventually the day came when he decided that he must leave his guardian and seek adventure. Gurnemanz was full of sorrow because, having no son to succeed him, he had hoped that Parzifal would stay and some day rule his land, and become the husband of his pretty daughter Liaze.

But Parzifal was ignorant of this poor man's hopes and rode away without a thought of the sadness he had left behind.

His journey was long and eventful. One day, after many weeks of travel, he came in sight of the mighty castle of Belrepeire. The castle lay under siege, for Queen Conwinamurs who ruled in this castle had no brave knights with whom to repel the

besiegers. The queen had inherited Belrepeire and many lands on her father's death, and now her whole kingdom was being laid waste by the greedy King Clamide. He wished to marry her and thereby gain for himself all this queen's lands.

Inside the castle the inhabitants were starving and near to surrender. However, when the queen's maid saw Parzifal approaching the castle, resplendent in his red and gold armour, she thought, 'Here is a worthy champion for my queen.'

Parzifal was secretly admitted and taken to the queen. To Conwinamurs he looked noble indeed. When Parzifal heard the full story of their plight he immediately set about mobilizing the castle's inhabitants so that when King Clamide's troops next attempted to scale the walls they would meet with showers of stones and boiling oil instead of meek surrender. As the days passed the queen became more

and more fond of Parzifal, and he of her, and soon she decided to marry him. Inside the castle everyone rejoiced as the marriage was celebrated.

King Clamide, sensing a new spirit in the besieged castle, went to the walls and issued a challenge to the knight who had breathed new life into the people of Belrepeire. But he was no match for Parzifal, who swiftly beat him. However, Parzifal did not slay him; instead, he ordered him to end the siege and leave Queen Conwinamurs' lands forever. Parzifal also put Clamide under oath to go to Arthur's court and offer to serve under the lady who had suffered blows for laughing at him.

Peace reigned in Queen Conwinamurs' kingdom, and for many months the couple lived in great happiness. But then Parzifal grew restless, for he remembered that he had still not been knighted. He decided to go once again to Arthur's court and be dubbed a knight. Conwinamurs was sad, yet she knew she could not prevent her husband from making this journey.

Once again Parzifal set out on his travels and after many months he reached a great forest close by King Arthur's court. It so happened that one of Arthur's pages was taking the king's favourite falcon out to exercise that day. Suddenly the falcon flew from the page's wrist where it had been perched. The page followed the bird: he could not see where it flew, but he could hear the sound of the little bell that was attached to the bird's foot. As he chased after the falcon, it led him to where Parzifal was.

The elements have the power to work strange magic, and even though it was summer the earth in this place was covered with a heavy fall of snow. As the sharp-eyed falcon flew through the air it spied a potential prey – three white flying geese. The falcon swooped and with its sharp beak pierced the breast of one of the geese. As the goose fell through the trees to the ground three drops of its blood dropped on to the newly-fallen snow. Parzifal saw these three drops and was transfixed, for he saw that the blood, mingling with the snow, resembled closely the skin, cheek and lips of his wife. He found himself lost to love and to thoughts of his absent wife.

When the page saw this knight standing motionless he immediately thought him to be a challenger to the knights of the Round Table, for Parzifal was holding his lance in rest as if ready for battle. Thinking of the good sport that such a combat would bring, the page, forgetting the falcon, ran helter-skelter back to the court where he breathlessly related what he had seen.

All the knights begged Arthur to allow them to go and meet this warlike knight. From the description of his armour, they realized that this must be the knight who had slain Sir Ither and sent King Clamide to Arthur's court. Every one of them was eager to try his skill against this renowned, yet unknown, knight. The first joust fell to Sir Segremore, a relative of Queen Guinevere, who had used his ties of kinship to the queen to persuade her to obtain Arthur's permission for him to fight first.

Sir Segremore rode out and found Parzifal, who was still magically transfixed, dreaming of his wife. He neither saw nor heard Sir Segremore's approach. Sir Segremore charged at the motionless knight. Yet when his lance hit Parzifal's shield it had no effect. However, Sir Segremore had charged with such force that he had been catapulted from his horse on impact and now lay helpless on the ground.

Sir Segremore's riderless horse returned to Arthur's court, and at once Sir Kay rode out to fight the mysterious knight. He found Parzifal still transfixed by the blood on the snow. When there was no reply to his challenge, Sir Kay interpreted Parzifal's silence as arrogance, and so he charged at a mighty gallop towards him. Sir Kay's mistake was soon apparent: he found himself on the receiving end of the unseeing knight's lance. The force of the impact unhorsed Sir Kay. He was hurled through the air, landing with a crash against a tree into which the slain white goose had fallen. Poor Sir Kay now lay on the ground with an arm and a leg broken.

When Sir Kay did not return, Sir Gawain set out. He quickly found Parzifal, still rooted to the spot, and like Sir Kay he received no reply to his greeting. But Sir Gawain followed the line of Parzifal's eye and saw the blood on the snow. Sir Gawain, too, had also suffered greatly from the torments of love, and he soon realized what afflicted this noble knight. Without more ado he threw his cloak over the blood, at which Parzifal's scattered wits were restored. Sir Gawain greeted Parzifal courteously and led him to King Arthur's court.

The whole court had turned out to welcome this knight, and when Parzifal revealed that he had not in fact been knighted, King Arthur immediately ordered preparations to be made for his initiation.

A wooden platform was hastily erected in the open so that all could see the ceremony take place. Squires helped Parzifal out of his armour and hurried to clean and polish it for the ceremony. Others led Parzifal to the bath-house where he was washed, his hair was cut, and he was dressed freshly in new linen garments. Flanked by many knights, he was led in pomp to the platform and, in full view, he was clad in his armour. As a special mark of favour Queen Guinevere and Lady Gunneware helped in this task. King Arthur, too, presented Parzifal with golden spurs and himself chose a jewelled sword for him from his armoury.

Finally, when Parzifal was fully dressed in his armour, the king girded on his sword, and Parzifal knelt to be dubbed a knight.

He had now fulfilled his greatest ambition. As he rose and turned to face the crowd, the cheers were deafening. And those cheers were justified, for Parzifal was to prove himself to be a peerless knight whose good deeds brought nothing but glory to the order of the Round Table.

INITIATION

A squire was eligible for knighthood when he reached the age of twenty-one. By the thirteenth century the initiation into knighthood had grown into an elaborate religious, almost mystical, ceremony – a far cry from the original Teutonic custom of girding a sword on a youth to mark his transition to manhood.

In times of peace the ceremony usually took place around a major Christian festival such as Easter or Whitsuntide, when it was hoped the weather would be fine enough for much of it to be held outdoors.

Usually several squires were dubbed at one ceremony. At the initiation of the future Edward II in 1306 his father proclaimed that all eligible squires seeking to be dubbed should come to London to share this honour with his son. Two hundred and seventy-six squires turned up and in the crush two were killed, several fainted and fighting broke out which had to be halted before the ceremony could continue.

The ritual of initiation began with a ceremonial bath the night before the dubbing. Even though the bath was primarily for cleanliness it came to be regarded as an act of purification – a second baptism. As the squires sat in wooden bath-tubs water would be poured over them. One chronicler tells us of squires who sat fully clothed in the tubs. The aspirants were then asked if they were ready for the water to wash away their former life. On making an affirmative reply, they were then drenched.

Next the young men had their beards and their heads shaved, an act that symbolized their submission to the will of God. Often they were understandably reluctant to lose all their hair, so only a token lock of hair was removed.

The squires were now ready to be dressed. Each was clothed in a new white tunic, symbolizing his purity, under which he would wear a smaller black tunic with black hose and shoes to remind him of death. Over this would be thrown a magnificent red cloak to show his nobility and his willingness to shed blood for his God and his Church. Finally a white belt was placed round his waist, denoting his chastity.

Now it was time for the young men to go to church, where they would spend the night in vigil. Placing their new arms on the altar steps, they would pass the night meditating on the ceremony to take place the next day. They were not allowed to sit but had to either stand or kneel throughout the night. Their sponsors or a priest would be at hand to give encouragement if the temptation to sleep became too great.

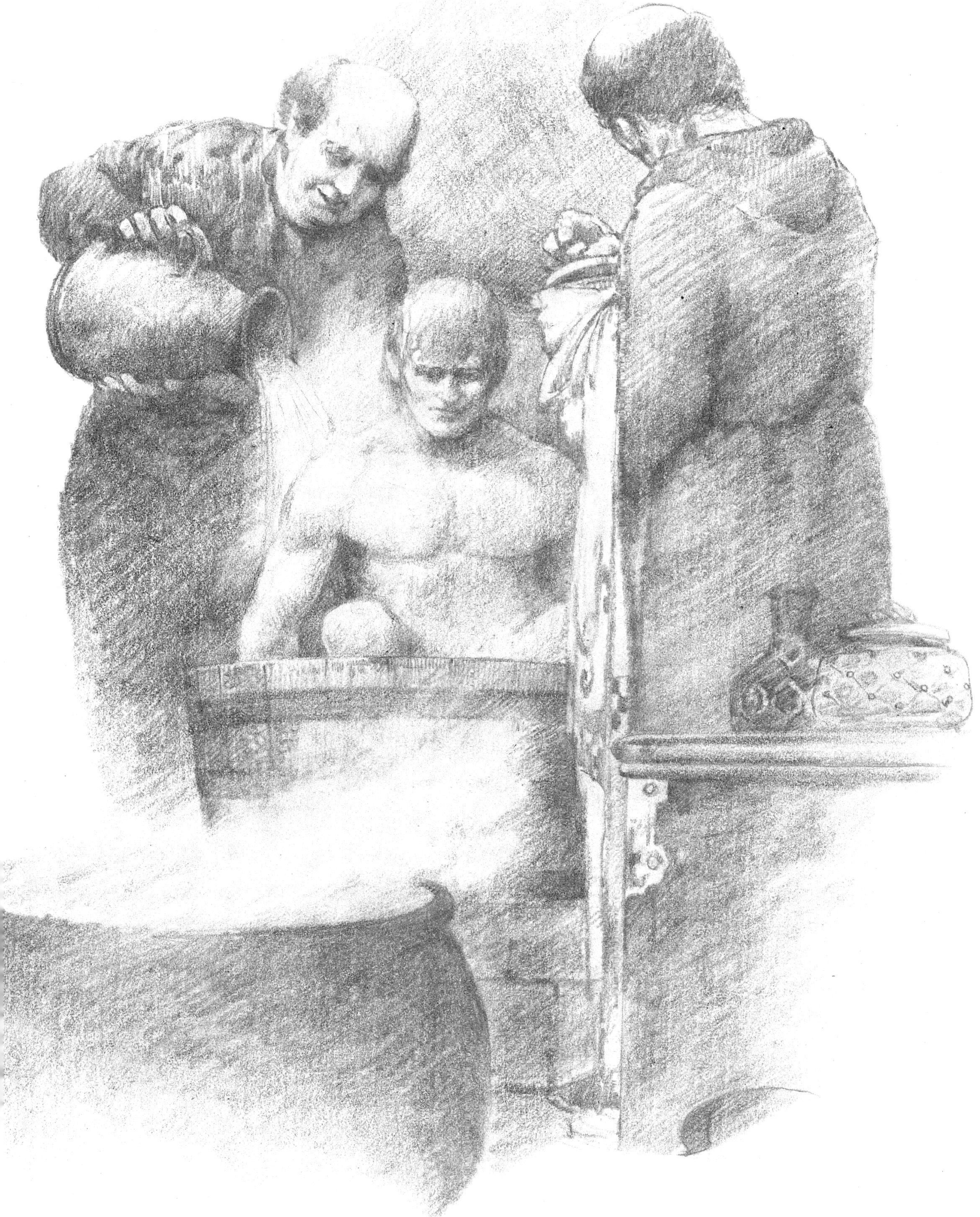

THE VIGIL

During the vigil the young man would have time to contemplate the duties and responsibilities of knighthood. He might also have repeated this prayer of initiation:

'Hearken we beseech Thee, O Lord, to our prayers, and deign to bless with the right hand of Thy Majesty this sword with which Thy servant desires to be girded, that it may be a defence of churches, widows, orphans and all Thy servants against the scourge of pagans, that it may be the terror and dread of all evil-doers, and that it may be just in both attack and defence.'

DUBBINGS

The actual initiation took place the following morning following the vigil. In the sight of the whole congregation gathered in the church the squire's sword and arms would be blessed. He would then progress to the place where the arming was to take place. His sponsor would fit on his armour. It was held to be auspicious if a woman helped with the arming of a knight, and even more so if the woman was the young man's fiancée. When armed with his hauberk, cuirasses and gauntlets he would then receive his golden spurs, the right one always being attached first. Finally the sword was girded on so that it hung on the knight's right side.

Fully armed, the new knight would kneel to receive the accolade, or colée, from his sponsor to remind him of the duties of knighthood. Originally this was a heavy blow delivered to the neck which could send the young man reeling. In time its force lessened to a gentle tap.

The ceremonious form of initiation was possible only in peace time, of course. In times of war men were often created knights on the battlefield, the words 'Be thou a knight' being sufficient ceremony. Such initiations gave rise to the plucking of three blades of grass, symbolizing the Blessed Trinity, to remind the new knight of his new role in life.

Sometimes squires were hastily dubbed before a battle to make up fighting numbers. The historian Froissart claimed that before the battle of Aljubarota, in 1385, 140 Spanish knights were created for this reason. This was doubtless a great morale-booster for the army, with so many new knights eager to do honour to their new station in life. Indeed, to be dubbed on the battlefield was often the only way an impoverished squire could gain a knighthood.

During the Hundred Years War a French squire, Regnault, captured the English Earl of Suffolk. When the Earl discovered that his captor was not a knight, though he was of gentlemanly birth, he dubbed him forthwith: only a knight could capture another knight.

The spirit of initiation was sometimes abused, however. On one occasion, three knights set out on an adventure which, for reasons unknown, needed a fourth knight to make up their numbers. Riding through the fields they came upon a hapless peasant quietly tending his crops. They seized and immediately dubbed the astonished man, then set him on a horse so that they could continue on their quest. Unfortunately it appears that the poor peasant, rather than the irresponsible knights, was punished for this action.

THE CID

According to the code of chivalry, the knight was bound to defend his honour with his life. Any insult against his good name and reputation was considered to bring dishonour on his whole family. The tradition of seeking vengeance almost destroyed the glorious career of Rodrigo de Bivar, the most famous and chivalrous knight in all Spain.

It had been apparent to everyone from his boyhood that Rodrigo would achieve great fame. He showed unusual skill in bearing arms and was seemingly without fear – indeed, so fearless that he had a lion for a pet. This beast felt instinctively that it could trust its master and would follow Rodrigo as meekly as a dog.

Spain at this time was frequently troubled by Moorish armies invading from North Africa. When Rodrigo became a knight he became famous for the campaigns he led against the pagan aggressors. Yet as a conqueror Rodrigo was renowned for his courtesy and gallantry towards his prisoners. Indeed, his captives honoured him giving him the Moorish name *el sidi* (the Cid), meaning the lord.

Rodrigo's reputation also won him a noble fiancée, Chimène, whose beauty and goodness was renowned throughout Spain. She was the daughter of the powerful Count of Gormaz, champion of the King of Castile. Everyone rejoiced at the forthcoming wedding, for it seemed only right that Spain's great hero should be married to such a noble bride. But theirs was by no means an arranged marriage, for no sooner had the couple met than they had fallen deeply in love.

Now Chimène was preparing her trousseau, for it had been agreed that they should marry as soon as Rodrigo returned from his latest campaign. Gorgeous robes made from Moorish silks which Rodrigo had won as booty had been made and Chimène herself sewed precious stones and pearls, Rodrigo's gifts to her, on to the dresses. Every day Chimène would go to the window of her chamber in the castle at Castile and look out hoping to see a messenger bringing her news of Rodrigo. As each day ended she would sit pensively by the open window looking out over the countryside, praying that the next day would bring Rodrigo back to her. However, the fates must have decided that this man had had too many blessings heaped upon him, for just when fortune seemed to favour him most Rodrigo met with a great disaster.

Rodrigo's father, Don Diego, was an old and feeble man. His greatest joy was to hear of his son's victories, and to tell everyone he met about them. However, when

he was at the court of the King of Castile his incessant praise of his son so enraged the Count of Gormaz that, even though their children were soon to be married, the hot-tempered knight struck Don Diego a blow which sent him reeling to the ground.

Don Diego immediately returned to his castle at Bivar, where he counted the days until his son returned from the wars.

No sooner had Rodrigo returned than he realized that some great disaster had befallen his father. Don Diego then told his son of the Count's insult.

'I am too old and frail to avenge my honour,' he reflected. 'You must do this for me. Our family will count for nothing in the eyes of all men if this insult goes unavenged.'

Rodrigo was dismayed, for if he fought the count and defeated him he would by so doing lose the love of Chimène.

Seeing his dilemma, Don Diego said: 'Remember, my son, to retrieve the honour of your family is a duty. For a knight love is but a pleasure which follows after duty.'

Rodrigo knew his father spoke the truth. Straight away he sought out the count and challenged him for the dishonour he had brought upon the house of Bivar. The challenge was accepted, and in the ensuing duel the count was slain by Rodrigo. Rodrigo's father told his son to return to the campaigns immediately, so that he could exonerate himself by noble deeds from punishment for killing the count. This Rodrigo did, and he left for the campaigns without seeing or sending word to Chimène. For he now feared that they could never be married.

Many months passed and the court of Castile received no news of how the wars against the Moors were proceeding. Chimène, still in deep mourning for her father, went to petition King Alfonso that Rodrigo should pay for the death of her father with his life.

'Sire,' said Chimène, 'since my father was not blessed with a son to avenge his death, I come to you to ask for vengeance. Rodrigo de Bivar must die for the murder he has committed.'

King Alfonso knew that what Chimène demanded was only just. He rose from his throne to deliver judgement. But as he was about to speak, a messenger rushed into the chamber and bowed before him.

He did not wait to be given leave to speak but poured out his message: 'Sire, I bring news of a great victory. The Cid has driven back the Moors from our land. My words cannot do justice to the great deeds he has done for this kingdom. Day after day he breathed new life into our army. Never once did he shrink from fighting in the heat of the battle. Indeed, we all felt ourselves invincible when we knew the Cid was on the battlefield. We sought to fight beside him as he cut through the hordes of

infidels. I do not lie when I say that in the last battle we fought he cut down three hundred Moors and the mere sight of him set the pagan hordes to flight.'

The messenger never paused for breath, so anxious was he to describe the great feats of his commander. But even as he spoke the Cid entered the hall. The court watched as the tall, travel-stained figure walked towards the king.

'I bring you victory,' he said, and turning towards the entrance to the chamber he signalled for his Moorish captives to be brought forward to do homage to King Alfonso. As Rodrigo looked round he paled, for then he saw Chimène. He felt his love for her surge again within him, yet he could not speak to her. The sight of her, dressed in robes of deep mourning, were a painful reminder to him of her father's death. Chimène, too, had looked towards him but quickly turned away and would not meet his gaze.

'All blessings on you, Rodrigo de Bivar, for the great service you have done our land,' said King Alfonso. 'Your return is timely. Sentence of death was about to be pronounced upon you for the slaying of the Count of Gormaz. However, our most valiant knight, your victory has more than absolved you from punishment for this crime.'

Before the king could continue Chimène cried out: 'Sire, is this justice? Shall Rodrigo live when, but for him, my father would have been alive to equal his feats? If I am not to have the life of my father's murderer in payment for his crime, I call upon

a man to retrieve my family's honour by fighting him to the death in single combat. Before this court I swear that I shall marry the man who fights for me. Heaven will then show the justice of my plea.'

King Alfonso had no alternative but to agree to Chimène's demand. He had loved the Count, who had been his champion for many years, but he also felt confident that there was no knight in all Spain capable of defeating Rodrigo.

At the court there was a knight named Don Sancho who had long loved Chimène. He now came forward and, kneeling before her, offered to be her champion. Chimène removed a black scarf from her robe and handed it to Don Sancho saying: 'God bless you for this deed, Don Sancho. Wear this colour, and whosoever hands it back to me shall be my husband.'

The king proclaimed that the contest should take place the next day. Rising from his throne, he left the chamber and all the court filed out after him.

Soon the chamber was empty save for Chimène and Rodrigo. Should they speak? How could they ignore each other when but a few months previously they were to have been man and wife? They did not know what to do. Yet each knew that if they were to speak their former love for each other would be rekindled, whatever the feelings of duty that now separated them. Yet tomorrow Rodrigo might well die at Chimène's command. Silently Chimène moved to leave the chamber. As she passed by Rodrigo she cast her eyes to the ground and whispered, 'Although I have no colour for you to wear in the contest tomorrow I ask you for the love you once bore me to fight for me in your heart. I too have struggled beneath the heavy weight that duty demands. Know that my vengeance causes me as much grief as your vengeance cost you.'

Without another word or glance she was gone from the chamber. Rodrigo was perplexed, but then jubilant: how could he ever have thought that he had lost Chimène's love?

Next day the whole court gathered to watch the contest. All were seated in covered stands overlooking the open ground where the two men were to fight. At each end of the ground stood racks of lances made ready for the combatants. The two men's horses were being given a final check by their squires.

Rodrigo and Don Sancho mounted their horses, rode out and stopped before the place where the king sat. The herald came forward to deliver the challenge, and the two men rode back to their respective ends to collect their lances for the first encounter.

The only sound to be heard was the ruffling of the stand's canopies and the flags fluttering in the breeze. Suddenly there was the thud of the horses' hooves as the two

men galloped forward to engage their lances. On impact both men's lances splintered. Quickly they rode back to their lists to collect fresh lances. They charged a second time, raising clouds of dust as their brightly-caparisoned horses galloped forward. Once more their lances broke on impact. Now, at close quarters, they drew their battle-axes and aimed blows at each other's heads. Each man fought with the desperation of a man who has nothing to lose by dying.

Then Don Sancho was knocked from his horse by a mighty blow. As he struggled to free himself from beneath his horse Rodrigo dismounted and, with a flourish, drew his bright sword. Don Sancho was immediately on his feet with sword drawn and the two men cut and thrust at each other with a terrifying ferocity.

Each man tried to protect himself with his shield. But soon the wooden frames of their stout shields were splintered and the taut animal skins which covered the frames were cut to shreds.

The crowd started to murmur, and before long they were shouting their encouragement to the two men. Chimène sat motionless, her face pale and revealing nothing of what she may have been feeling.

At last Don Sancho seemed to tire, and sensing this Rodrigo attacked with renewed vigour until Don Sancho could hardly raise his sword to defend himself. He fell to the ground, at which Rodrigo swiftly placed the sharp point of his sword at Don Sancho's throat. Don Sancho's fingers slipped from his sword and with a feeble movement of his other hand he acknowledged that he was conquered.

Rodrigo drew his dagger with its long, slender blade. Everyone waited for Rodrigo to deliver the death blow. But he hesitated.

'Dona Chimène, here lies your champion,' proclaimed Rodrigo. 'His life is in your hands. Shall he live or die?'

Chimène raised her hand to indicate that he should be spared. Rodrigo immediately sheathed his dagger and bent to remove Chimène's by now bloodstained colour from Don Sancho's helmet. He walked to the stand and handed it up to Chimène.

'My lady, I return your favour. You promised that the man who returned it to you should be your husband and I now claim my prize. Chimène, I love you and have always loved you.'

At these words tears flowed from Chimène's eyes and she answered, 'I love you too.' Now vengeance had been seen to be done and there was no longer any impediment to their marriage.

Rodrigo and Chimène were soon married and their love grew with the passing years. Chimène would not be separated from her husband and even when Rodrigo was twice sent into exile, due to the jealousy of lesser men, she went with him.

The Cid lived to a great age but even as an old man he remained a great warrior. The Moors continued their campaigns against Spain, and at last held the Cid besieged in the city of Valencia. Day by day, fresh hordes of Moors were drawn up to the walls of the city, and the situation looked grave for the Spaniards. Then the Cid had a dream in which it was revealed to him that within thirty days he would die. Knowing his death would mean the fall of the city he conceived a plan. He instructed his officers that if he should die his body was to be strapped upright on his horse so that he could, for the last time, lead his army out of the besieged city. In great distress, his officers agreed.

The Cid's dream proved true and his men did as he had instructed them. For the

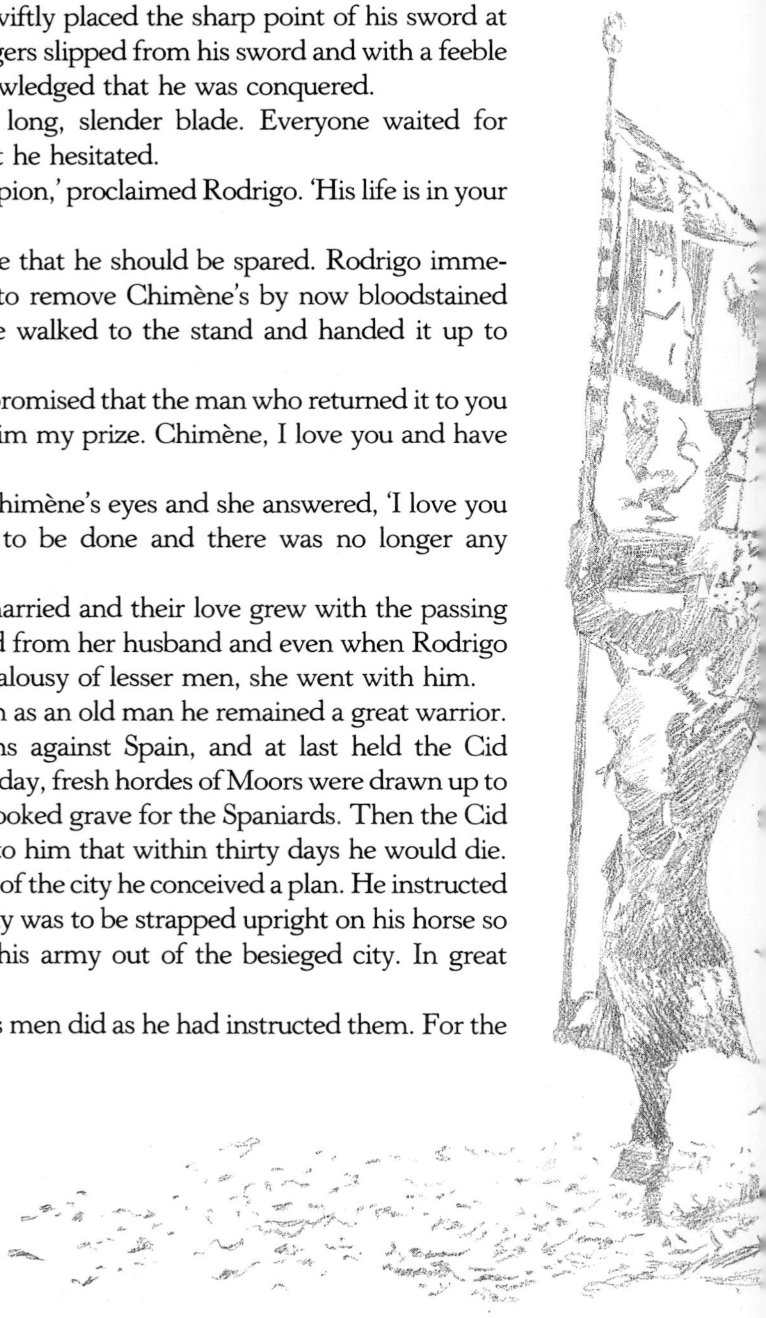

last time the Cid, mounted on his horse Bavieca, rode out at the head of his army – seemingly as brave and vital as he had ever been. The Moor's spies in Valencia had reported that the Cid's life was ended, and when the Moorish warriors saw him riding out of the city they were convinced that he had risen from the dead. In terror the Moors took to their ships and sailed back to North Africa.

The people of Valencia could not bear to bury their leader. For the next ten years his body sat, perfectly preserved, in the cathedral of Valencia. Finally it was interred in a magnificent tomb, and the great knight rests forever more beneath its stone.

THE CASTLE

The knight's castle, with its thick stone walls, was built primarily for defence. Its gateway was heavily fortified, being the obvious target for attack. An extra tower, known as the barbican, was built beyond the gatehouse. If attackers passed through this defence and reached the gatehouse the portcullis, a heavy iron grating, would be lowered. If somehow attackers got into the gatehouse before this had happened, they might suddenly find themselves trapped in a cage created by the lowering of portcullises at each end of the gatehouse. Invaders might then be killed by arrows fired through small slits ('murder holes') in the gatehouse wall.

The castle's spiral staircases were also designed for defence: a man climbing up the stairway could not see what was around the corner – an advantage for the defender. Boobytrap floors were also built, so that unwelcome visitors could be unceremoniously dumped into the dungeons which lay, below ground-level, at the bottom of towers.

The plan of a castle built on a linear design. By the twelfth century stone castles had replaced the earlier wooden castles. In medieval Germany 10,000 stone castles could be found. The thickness of the walls denoted a knight's wealth: one castle had walls 22 feet thick.

Our medieval ancestors loved to be surrounded by bright colours. Drab stone interior walls were painted in red or yellow ochre, or hung with tapestries. The White Tower at the Tower of London was once painted a brilliant white. In making their castles habitable knights would also make use of whatever items were freely available. Floors and walls, especially those of the bedchamber, were covered with animal skins. Whole tree trunks would burn in the large fireplaces. Flowers and herbs would be sprinkled on the rush-strewn floors to sweeten the air.

It is easy to appreciate why, at the slightest excuse or opportunity, provided there was no threat of attack, a knight would leave his castle. There was very little for him to do there as it was largely managed by his wife. He was, in fact, redundant, and more often than not got in the way. Moreover, these stone castles, with their small, glassless windows, were hot and airless in summer. In winter the castle was cold and draughty, and though there was always plenty of wood for fires there was no adequate chimney to take away the smoke. The only light was usually from reeds placed in a dish of oil – a smoky, smelly and not over-effective lamp. Little importance was attached to cleanliness: the remains of all the meals eaten and other debris which had fallen on the rushes covering the floor was left there far longer than it should have been.

Furniture was usually minimal: probably the lord of the castle would have been the only person who slept in a bed. At the foot of this would be a heavy chest, kept locked, in which he stored family treasures and other valuables.

The place where a castle was built was chosen solely for reasons of defence. Set either on a natural or a man-made mound, the castle was surrounded by a deep ditch, often filled with water to make a moat. A castle built on a concentric plan, with a curtain wall built round the perimeter of the whole edifice, was the strongest design. At first stones were removed from the top of the curtain wall to give protection to defenders when repelling attackers. In time stone protrusions or machicolations were built at this point. These defences had no floors, so that once behind the machicolations the defenders could safely discharge missiles or pour boiling oil down on to the enemy.

THE SIEGE

A siege could be a very tedious business for a knight, sometimes lasting several years. Knights never involved themselves with the mechanics of the siege. They took an active part only when the hand-to-hand fighting began. To alleviate boredom they would arrange a diversion with the enemy called 'fighting at the barriers'. A wooden barrier was erected at the castle's gates and the knights would lunge at each other through this. In keeping with the code of chivalry, strict rules of conduct would be observed during this contest so that no surprise attack could be launched at the castle. At other times besieging knights would devastate the surrounding countryside, which probably belonged to the knight they were attacking.

There were three stages in a siege. First the besieging commander would call to the castle to surrender: if there was no surrender, the castle walls were reconnoitred to find a point at which a breach could be made. Professional siege engineers were employed to conduct this operation, drawing up plans and devices for undermining the walls.

Next the footsoldiers attempted to scale the walls. This always resulted in numerous casualties as missiles, boiling oil and quicklime (to burn and blind) would rain down on the assailants. But these men, unlike the knights, were expendable. The final stage was the drawing up of the siege machines to breach the walls, by now undermined. Volleys of rocks, boulders and stones, which shattered like shrapnel on impact, would be hurled at the castle. Sometimes a dead horse was launched into the castle to spread disease. To demoralize the besieged, prisoners, or captured spies, were sometimes jettisoned, like human cannonballs, into the castle. Barrels alight with burning rags were also launched to set the castle on fire.

Nevertheless, until the discovery of gunpowder in the fourteenth century those within the castle had the upper hand in sieges. If they could resist the assaults, maintain supplies of food and water and remain patient, they would usually be victorious, unless a traitor, or spy on the inside, provided the enemy with valuable information or, worse, secretly admitted them.

The siege tower or **beffroy** was a favourite weapon of Richard the Lionheart. Besiegers could make a direct assault on a castle by drawing the tower up to the walls. However it was very heavy and difficult to move.

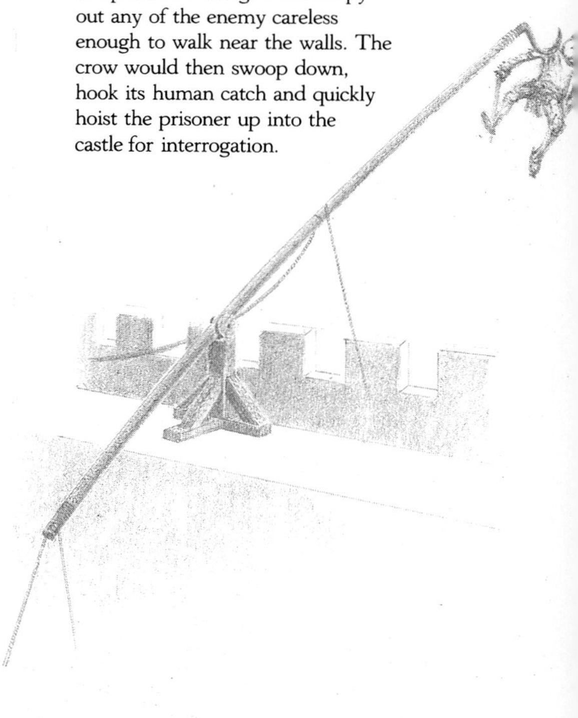

The crow worked on the principle of a giant fulcrum with a large hook at one end. From their vantage point on the castle's ramparts the besieged would spy out any of the enemy careless enough to walk near the walls. The crow would then swoop down, hook its human catch and quickly hoist the prisoner up into the castle for interrogation.

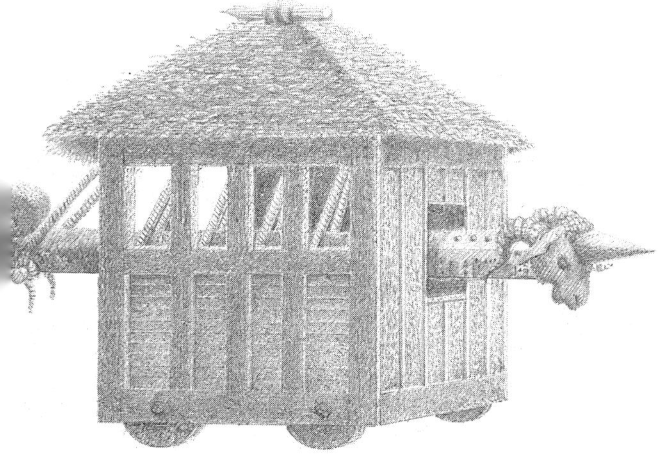

The battering ram was used to pick holes in castle walls. Often a protective 'house' was erected over the soldiers manning the battering ram. This often collapsed under the weight of stones hurled down on to its roof. The besieged often lowered bales of straw or cotton to come between the ram and the castle's walls to lessen the blows' effectiveness.

Another means of rendering the battering ram ineffective. However, fire-arrows fired at its protective 'house' were probably the best way to unman the battering ram.

The magonel was a less sophisticated form of trebuchet. When released the long arm could hurl projectiles weighing up to 200 lbs at the castle's walls.

The trebuchet, the largest siege weapon, contained heavy weights at one end. When the arm was released the weight swung the arm up throwing the projectiles from the sling at the other end. Often the ropes were made of human hair. But if the weather was wet the rope slackened and lost its efficiency. The trebuchet's aim was not very accurate.

For seven long years the Emperor Charlemagne had waged war against the Moors in Spain. Now he had conquered all the land save for the mountain city of Saragossa where the pagan king Marsilion had taken refuge. In a garden within this besieged city, King Marsilion called his wisest men together to ask how he might rid Spain of Charlemagne and his mighty army so he might rule in that land once again.

Blancadrin, the wisest of all his counsellors, spoke: 'Great King, pretend to submit to Charlemagne. Send him gifts, and tell him that you will become a Christian and be his vassal when he returns to France. Also, send him your sons as hostages. Do all these things and Charlemagne will return across the mountains to France and disband his army. Once this has been done we can rule again in Spain.'

Marsilion listened to this advice and said: 'Blancadrin, I like your plan. Therefore go to Charlemagne's camp and tell him that if he leaves Spain within the month I will give him safe passage into France. This done, tell him also that I will myself go to his court at Aix and be baptised and promise to be his vassal.'

Blancadrin departed, and in his train he brought with him fine gifts for the Emperor, including coffers of jewels and gold, lions, bears and falcons – all to show that he came in good faith.

When Charlemagne and his nobles had heard King Marsilion's terms they thought carefully. In the past all attempts to make peace had failed and it seemed strange that the pagan king now seemed prepared to surrender to his enemy. Some of the nobles feared it was but a trick to deceive the emperor, and they argued that the war should continue until all the Moors had been driven from Spain.

Foremost of this opinion was Roland, the Emperor's nephew. 'Do not believe these words,' he said, 'for once we have left Spain the Moors will reconquer all the lands we have struggled for seven years to win. Are we to forget all our knights who have died in this war?' Charlemagne took heed, for of all his knights he loved Roland the best.

Roland's stepfather Ganilon was the next to speak: 'Why continue this war when peace is offered to us? Only a proud fool would continue this war, and what need have we of fools?'

The oldest and the wisest of Charlemagne's knights agreed with what Ganilon

said. Charlemagne finally agreed to accept King Marsilion's terms and looked among his knights for one to act as ambassador to the Moorish king.

'Let it be me,' said Roland. 'If I may not meet the infidel with my sword, let me at least meet him with your words.'

'No, Roland,' said his good friend Oliver. 'You are too hot-headed and proud to undertake such a delicate mission. I fear your quick temper would lead you into trouble.'

Roland bristled at these words and exclaimed mockingly, 'Then send my stepfather Ganilon. Let Ganilon go to the Moorish king since he is such a lover of peace.'

However, everyone thought Ganilon a good choice for he had the reputation of being a prudent man.

Ganilon was furious, for this was a dangerous mission. The last two ambassadors sent to King Marsilion had been tortured and finally beheaded. Why, Ganilon thought, should my stepson suggest that I go unless he wishes me ill? He vowed silently that if he returned safely from this mission he would never rest until he had brought about the death of Roland.

Ganilon rode towards Saragossa, side by side with Blancadrin. This cunning man had noticed Ganilon's anger towards Roland, and as he talked to him he discovered just how jealous Ganilon was of his stepson. Blancadrin saw this knight was ripe for treachery, and as they continued their journey the two men plotted and finally devised a plan to bring about the destruction of Roland.

When they reached Saragossa King Marsilion was surprised to find this Christian knight so ready to betray his fellow countrymen. Yet he listened carefully to Ganilon as he told him of his plan. His lips curled in an evil smile for in it he saw how Charlemagne's bravest warriors might be destroyed.

'Do exactly as you promised, Charlemagne,' urged Ganilon. 'Within the month he will return to France, for he is old and longs to leave this war and live out his days in peace. He will return to France leaving only a small rearguard to protect the main army as he passes through the mountains. This, I swear, will be commanded by Roland and Charlemagne's most courageous knights. Attack this troop with the full

strength of your army and you cannot fail to destroy it. Charlemagne will never return to fight you for you will have killed his best fighting men, the very flower of his army. He will no longer have the will or the force to fight you.'

Finally Ganilon told the Moors the very spot from which to attack the rearguard: the narrow valley of Roncesvalles. In payment for his treason Ganilon was showered with gold and jewels from the king's treasury.

Ganilon returned to Charlemagne's camp and told the Emperor, 'The Moors will give you a safe passage into France and within a month Marsilion will come to your court, be baptized and be your vassal.'

Charlemagne was pleased and immediately gave orders to break camp and prepare to return to France. His men were joyful for they longed to go back to their homeland, and see their families again.

Charlemagne asked for a knight to command the rearguard.

Quickly Ganilon spoke: 'Let it be Roland.'

All agreed that there was no better knight to undertake this command. As a special mark of his esteem for Roland, Charlemagne allowed him to choose the knights who should make up this force. As Ganilon had anticipated, he chose the most courageous warriors of the emperor's whole army.

Walker

The mighty army set forth. Soon the steep mountain passes rang with the hooves of thousands of horses and thousands of pennons fluttered in the breeze. Slowly, taking up the rear, came Roland and his loyal band of knights, frequently glancing behind them in case of any sudden attack.

But they could not know that at that very moment Marsilion's army was advancing stealthily towards them on horses with muffled hooves and all their glittering armour hidden from the light. For as the emperor's army passed across the mountain paths, the pagan hordes stole by secret ways to the ridges above the steep-sided valley into which the French army's march would lead them.

The army marched all through the day and all through the night and as dawn was breaking they entered into the valley of Roncesvalles. Soon the main body had passed through to safety.

Dawn had broken as Roland rode into the valley. As his eyes searched the wooded slopes he thought he saw the morning sun glitter strangely among the trees. Suddenly the slopes blossomed with pagan banners and Roland saw before him the assembled might of the enemy.

His proud face grew bright with fury at the pagan's treachery. He realized then that he must have been betrayed, for only one of his countrymen could have known the route that Charlemagne would have taken through this valley – and that traitor must be Ganilon. Quickly he turned to warn his companions to prepare for the attack.

'Sound your horn while there is still time and let Charlemagne know we are under attack,' said Oliver.

'Never,' said Roland. 'Never shall men say that Christian knights trembled before the pagan's might. If we must die, our death will be for the glory of God.'

But even as they spoke, the first wave of the pagan hordes, their crimson, white and blue pennants streaming from the points of their spears, spilled down the hillside.

The warrior Archbishop Turpin set down his mace and hastily blessed the knights. Roland rode to the front of his men, mounted on his horse Veillantif.

Brandishing his sword, Durendal, he cried, 'Advance, brave companions! Give the pagans the death they seek.'

Drawing their swords, this small troop filled the air with their war cry, '*Mountjoye!*', and galloped forward to meet the enemy.

The courageous French knights rode fearlessly through the pagan hordes, striking down all who stood in their way and cutting through coats of mail with what seemed like superhuman strength.

Four times fresh waves of Moors came down the hillside, and four times the knights held their own against the attack. The battle raged on and still the cry of '*Mountjoye!*' rose above the din of the dreadful fighting. The once green grass now ran red with blood and the corpses of many warriors lay all around.

King Marsilion, surveying the carnage, had his trumpets sound. At this note his choicest band of warriors rode forward. Dazzling with jewelled helmets and golden armour, covered with saffron surcoats, this troop advanced to attack the battle-weary French.

The French knights bravely fought this fresh wave of warriors but soon only twenty of the knights remained alive.

'Blow your horn, Roland,' begged Oliver. Yet still Roland refused to do so. Then Archbishop Turpin, who had fought as well as any knight that day, rode up.

'Blow your horn, Roland. Death is now certain, but you should at least let our kinsmen know so that we may receive a Christian burial,' said Archbishop Turpin.

Roland took his horn and sounded a blast. Then he blew a second time, more loudly, at which the carrion crows hovering over the bloody bodies on the battlefield rose into the air. Then he blew a third time, louder still, and so great was his effort that blood spilt from his mouth.

The sound travelled far across the mountains and was heard by Charlemagne: 'Surely that is Roland's horn?' he asked.

'No,' answered the traitor Ganilon, who was riding with the emperor. 'It is only a hunter's horn.' Then the horn was heard again.

'Roland is in distress,' said Charlemagne. Then, when he heard the third blast he knew for certain that Roland had been attacked and needed help. He turned towards Ganilon and saw his look of guilt and straight away had him bound in chains and led away.

Charlemagne immediately gave orders to return to Roncesvalles. Through the rocky mountains and along the steep ravines the army, filled with dread, retraced their steps as quickly as they could.

By now only three of the vanguard remained alive – Roland, Oliver and Archbishop Turpin. Still the Moors came on in droves. Then Oliver was struck by a blow which sent him reeling and blinded his eyes with blood. Roland, seeing him hurt, rode frantically, striking down pagans as he went, to aid his friend. Unable to see who was coming towards him, Oliver lashed out wildly with his sword and struck Roland a fatal blow.

'What has possessed you? Oliver, do you not know me? It is I, Roland.'

'I hear but do not see you brother,' said Oliver, and sensing that he might have struck his friend, he said, 'Forgive me if I have harmed you.' These were the last words Oliver spoke.

The Moors now withdrew to rest, thinking all the French knights had been slain. But Roland slowly made his way to where he could see a lone tree. He came upon the body of Archbishop Turpin and realized that he alone remained alive. Slipping from his horse he lay down on the ground. His wound was causing him great pain, but after a moment he struggled to sit up, lifted his horn to his lips and blew a feeble note. Across the mountains the air sounded with the answering notes of a thousand clarions. Hearing that, he smiled, for now he knew that his death would not go unavenged.

Roland felt death approaching but even at this moment he saw another pagan was advancing on him. The new adversary tried to take his sword as he lay helpless on the ground. Gathering what remained of his strength, Roland cut down this man, and with a last effort hurled his sword against a rock to shatter it, so that no pagan should hold his sword, Durendal. But the steel of the blade would not break. Then he took his sword and, sinking to the ground, he placed it with the tip of the blade pointing towards Spain to show Charlemagne he had not turned from the enemy. So Roland died.

When Charlemagne reached the valley he shook with rage at the sight which awaited him. Without a moment's delay, he ordered his army to attack the Moors. His army fell upon the pagans, eager to avenge their comrades who had been so treacherously slain. Like the tide which rushes without check to the shore, Charlemagne's army overran the Moors. With tireless strength, the French army drove forward to the city of Saragossa and razed it to the ground. Still the French fought, putting to the sword all the stragglers of Marsilion's army until it was destroyed.

Then the sorrowful army returned to France. As they passed through the countryside on their sad journey to Charlemagne's capital, Aix-la-Chapelle, the people wept to see the bodies of the slaughtered knights being carried home in state for burial. But the glory won by these warriors and their commander, the peerless knight Roland, shall never be forgotten.

HELMETS

As the head was the most exposed and vulnerable part of the knight's body, the helmet was the most important part of any knight's armour. Helmets were made by highly-skilled ironsmiths, who would vary the thickness of the iron at places on the helmet most likely to be hit.

Helmets were rarely comfortable. They were heavy – some helmets weighed as much as 25 lbs. The head had to bear much of this weight, so to ease the pressure on the head, and to lessen the risk of concussion from blows knights would bandage their heads or wear, underneath the helmet, a close-fitting leather cap padded with either straw or cotton.

Knights would always wait until the last possible moment before donning their helmets. Once the helmet was on, it was very difficult for the knight to hear. He would also find it hard to talk or to give commands, he could not wipe away perspiration and, if a blow knocked his helmet askew, he would be unable to see. On more than one occasion a knight knocked from his horse while still wearing his helmet is said to have drowned in a couple of inches of water.

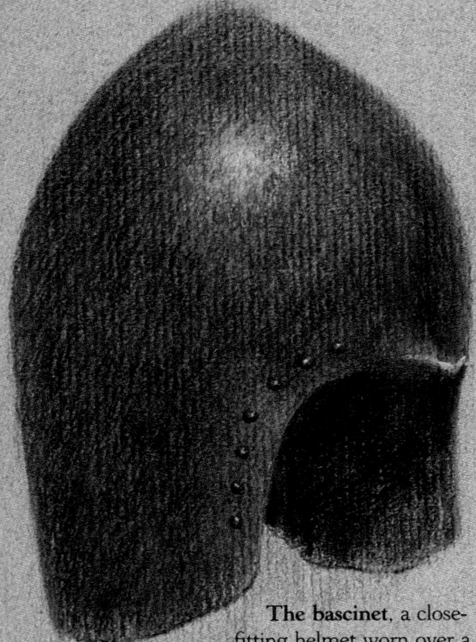

The bascinet, a close-fitting helmet worn over a hood, or *coif*, of chain mail. The conical shape of the crown, together with the smooth and rounded edges of the helmet, made it difficult for cutting or thrusting weapons to find a sure hold on the helmet.

The salade, a hat-shaped helmet, was very popular because it was relatively lightweight and comfortable to wear. The back of the helmet was elongated to protect the neck while the chin guard protected the front of the face.

The helm, a flat-topped helmet which rested on the wearer's shoulders: when wearing this helmet the knight could only breathe through the narrow eye-slits and holes on the front.

The armet, a very close-fitting helmet, could only be worn by first opening it then assembling the various pieces, using rivets, around the knight's head.

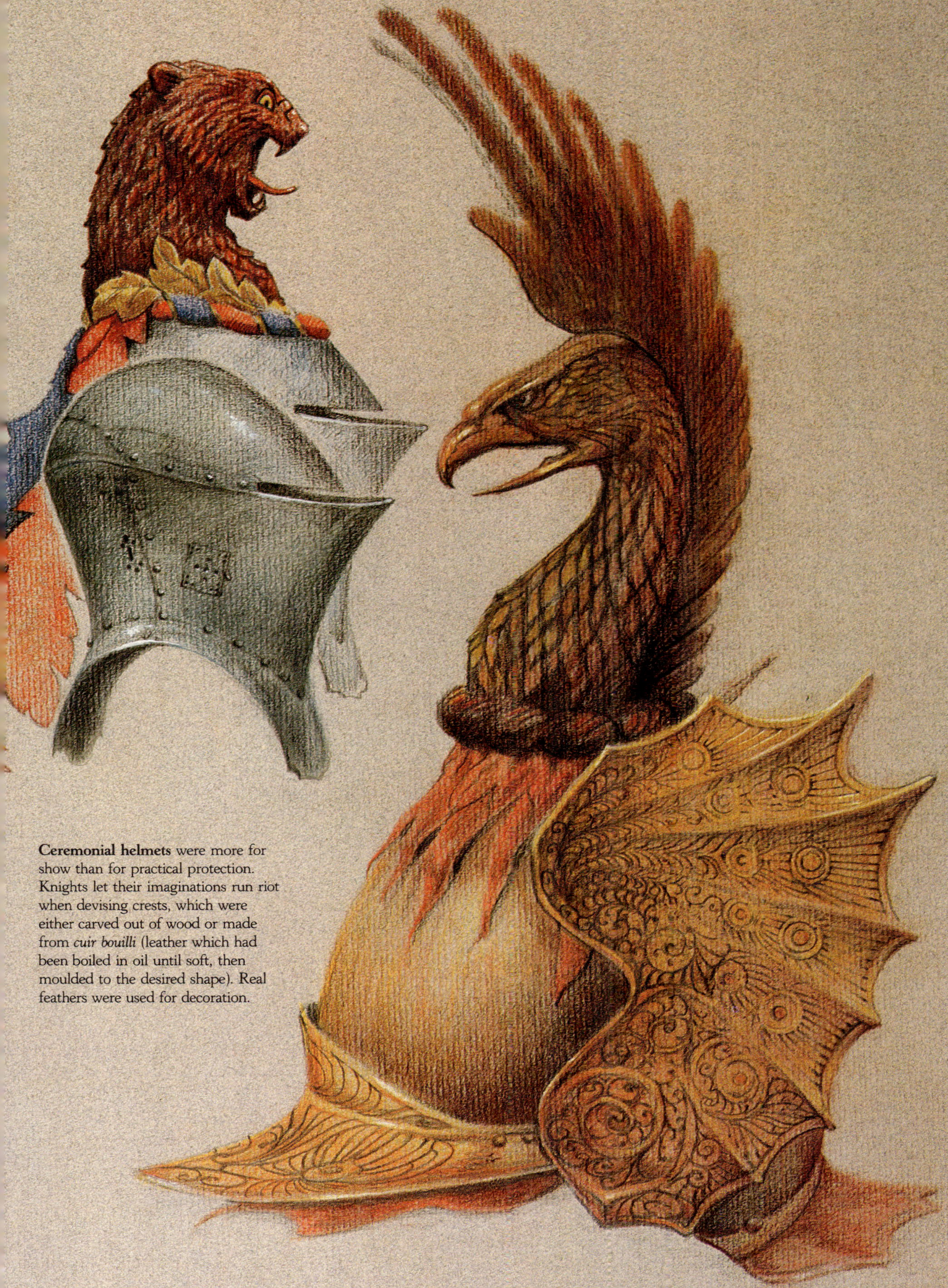

Ceremonial helmets were more for show than for practical protection. Knights let their imaginations run riot when devising crests, which were either carved out of wood or made from *cuir bouilli* (leather which had been boiled in oil until soft, then moulded to the desired shape). Real feathers were used for decoration.

ARMOUR

The knight's role as a warrior meant that his survival depended on how well he was protected from sword thrusts, blows from battle-axes and flying arrows.

Until the mid-fourteenth century the hauberk, made of chainmail, was the main body protection. Weighing up to 30 lbs, the hauberk was made of interlinked metal rings, and often comprised over 200,000 links. It was very flexible and easy to put on – it simply slipped over the head – and could be carried, rolled up, behind the saddle.

However, as defensive clothing it was not perfect. The edge of a sword would bite against the mail and although the rings would not break, the blow would certainly bruise the wearer. To lessen this effect knights wore a gambeson, a garment thickly padded with felted hair or cotton to prevent chafing, next to his skin. Arrows would stick to the chain mail. Crusading knights often emerged from encounters with infidels uninjured but bristling like porcupines with arrows embedded in their chainmail.

To improve their armour's protective qualities knights began to introduce metal plates into the mail, especially at the elbows and knees, so that they could bend their limbs even when encased in mail. Plates of metal introduced to protect shins and forearms were then enlarged, hinged at one side and held in place with rivets or straps.

Eventually the knight was completely encased in plate armour. Enormous skill went into its making. Beating out a single ingot, the armourer would leave individual pieces thicker at the more vulnerable places. Such armour had to be made to measure, so surviving suits give an intriguing idea of what the man who wore it looked like, whether, for example, he was long-limbed, pot-bellied or had large feet. It appears that knights often had rather undeveloped calf muscles as most of the shin guards are too small for any man now to wear with comfort. This feature of the knight's physique complies with the knight's conviction that in accordance with his station in life he should ride everywhere: walking was only for the lower orders.

Mounted on his horse and clad in his plate armour, a knight was virtually impregnable, for the smooth, rounded edges of the armour deflected all blows. Nevertheless it took hours to don this plate armour: the night before a battle was frequently spent arming. Knights in full armour would often have to be lowered by means of a pulley on to their horses. Once knocked from his horse, the knight resembled, and was as helpless as, a beached lobster. A stranded knight was often the victim of footsoldiers, who would kill him either by hacking at his armour, beating him to death or stabbing him through the joins in the plate.

Chainmail rusted and tarnished very quickly. For cleaning, the coat of mail was placed in a leather sack with a mixture of sand and vinegar. This was sealed and tossed strenuously until the mail was cleaned.

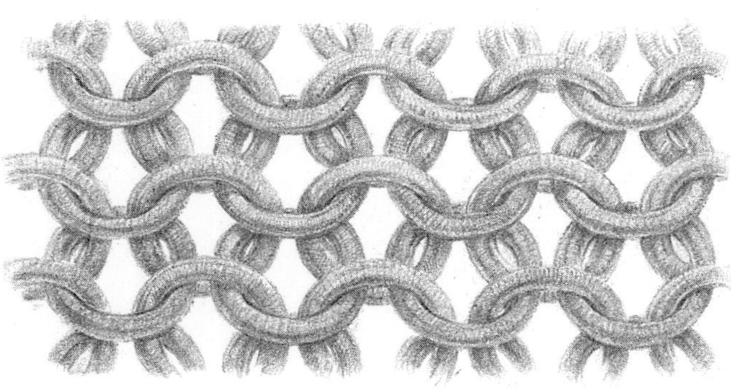

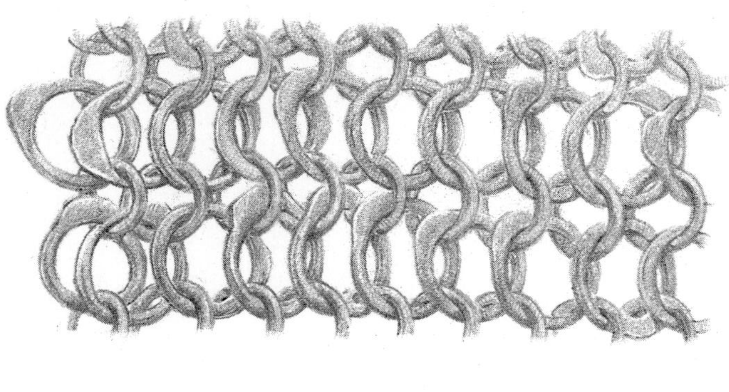

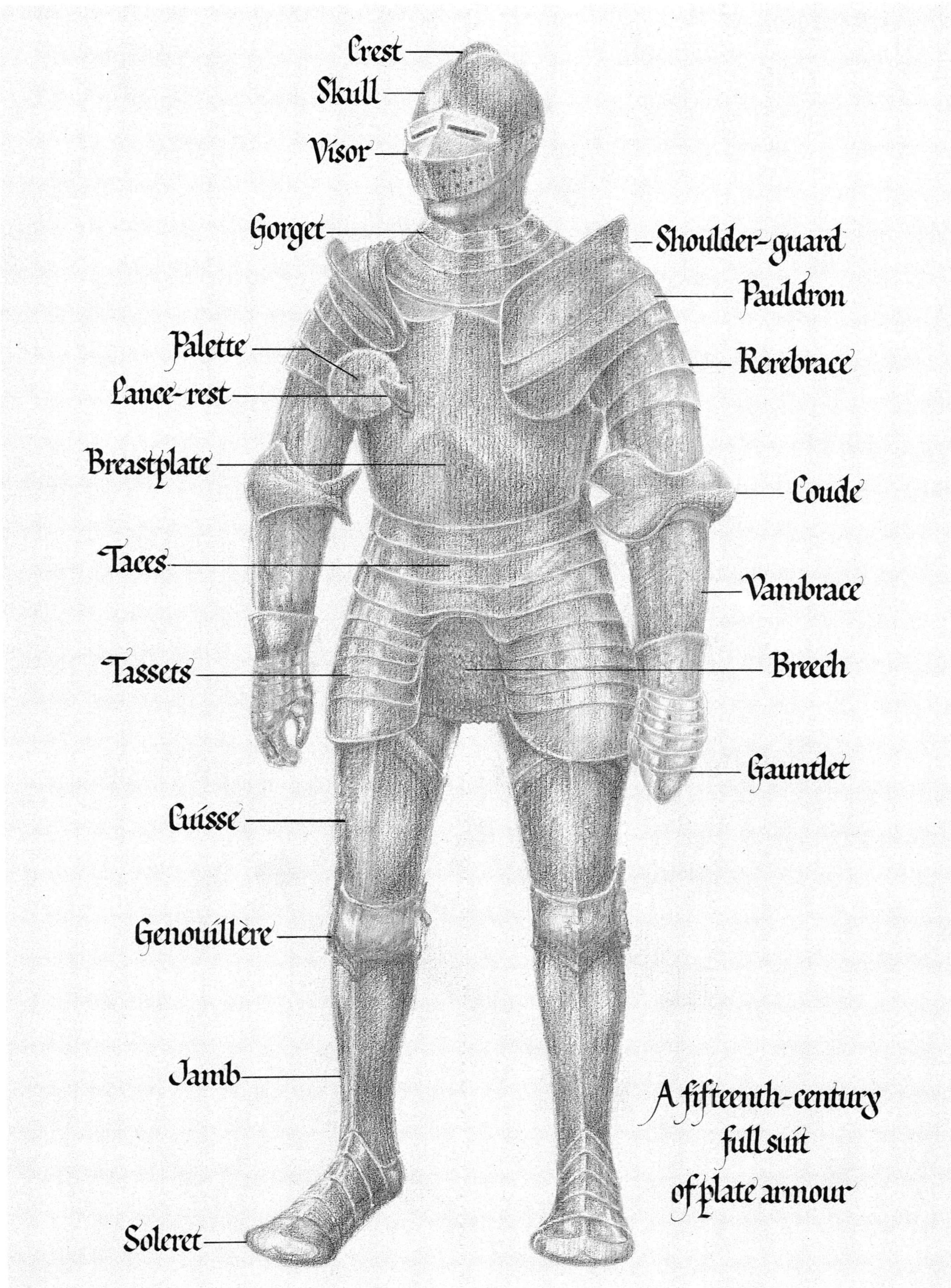

A fifteenth-century full suit of plate armour

THE HORSE

The knight's horse set him, in more than one sense, above other men. Together with his sword, it was his most prized possession. The figure of the mounted warrior quickly came to symbolize power and authority.

The knight's pre-eminence as an armed horseman was also due to the fact that he could remain seated on his horse. The saddle with its raised cantle at the back and pommel in the front gave him a secure seat. The use of stirrups, originating in China, also enabled him to move quickly and remain in the saddle.

To the knight the horse became almost an heroic figure and in medieval romances horses such as Roland's Veillantif and the Cid's Bavieca were as famed as their riders. Knights cared no less for their own horses: often they gave them names which expressed their characteristics, such as Baucent meaning 'white socks', Fauvel meaning 'tawny' or Brigliadore, to commemorate the horse's golden bridle. Each knight would equip his horse as lavishly as his wealth allowed, often hanging small, golden, jangling bells from its harness. Horses were frequently the coveted prize for the victor of a tournament or battle.

On campaigns, such as a crusade, the knight would share his tent at night with his horse, and if water was in short supply he would see that his horse was the first to have something to drink. There is one most uncharacteristic story of a knight who burnt alive thirty of his horses for a bet, but otherwise nothing but kindness, was shown by knights to their steeds.

A knight usually had three horses: for everyday purposes he had a couple of palfreys, strong yet elegant horses; his warhorse, the destrier, was specially bred to withstand the clash of battle and to bear the weight of a fully-armoured knight. The massively proportioned destrier was also armoured, sometimes so heavily that they were unable to move.

The destrier, always an ungelded stallion so that it retained its natural ferocity, had to be kept in a separate field because it would otherwise attack other horses. It was specially trained, usually by the squire, to respond to leg commands so that in battle its rider's arms would be left free to fight. However, despite its great strength and useful ability to trample on the enemy the destrier lacked stamina. It could not sustain a gallop but could, at best, trot. This was apparently most uncomfortable for the rider. Indeed, the Teutonic knights devised an unpleasant punishment for miscreants – an hour's trotting, in full armour, on a destrier.

THE KNIGHT IN PERSON

The medieval knight was probably not far removed in physique from his twentieth-century counterpart. He was perhaps a little shorter, with broad shoulders and strong arms, and undoubtedly robust, for not only did he take a great deal of physical exercise but also he had survived his medieval childhood, with its constant threat of diseases such as typhus, cholera, smallpox and infection from wounds, polluted water and vermin.

The close proximity of death (the average life-expectancy for those who survived to adulthood was only thirty to thirty-five years) certainly made men more superstitious. Knights believed implicitly in omens and predictions and tried to protect themselves by wearing religious medallions and carrying holy relics on their journeys.

Blindness, caused by disease, was far more common than it is today, but this was seemingly no major hindrance, as the blind King of Bohemia tried to show when he rode into battle on his horse led by two knights. Not surprisingly, the king was killed in the battle.

Knights were very vain about their appearance, but it was their own opinion of their appearance which counted more than reality. One knight ravaged a neighbour's land after receiving what he considered to be a slur against his looks. In fact, knights bore the marks of their lifestyle: scars, scratches, slit noses, missing ears and teeth – legacies of a lifetime of fighting.

But knights took some care with their looks. Some knights, no doubt well-groomed, were even chosen as 'pin-ups', as spinning songs sung by women during the Crusades reveal. They would permit their hair to be combed, washed and oiled. Some even had their hair curled with hot tongs, and they were not above having their hair hennaed to improve its lustre. However, it was no pleasure for a knight to have his hair cut because scissors at this time were rather like crude garden shears which did not cut cleanly.

Many contemporary pictures show clean-shaven knights. Shaving must have been an uncomfortable procedure, for razors then resembled giant carving knives and there was no hot water or soap. But beards did have their vogue, and in twelfth-century France there was a fashion for wearing small, tufted beards into which knights wove little strands of gold thread.

Contrary to popular belief knights took baths frequently. It was often the only way to relax after many hours in the saddle wearing armour, or to ease the bruises and grazes received in fights. It also eased the discomfort from flea-bites, which were part and parcel of living in a castle. When visitors arrived at a castle they would immediately be offered a bath and a change of clothes. The medieval bath resembled a wooden tub with a seat in it, on which the knight would sit while hot, perfumed or oiled water was poured round him. It was not uncommon for young women to attend the knight in his bath.

Knights were not so particular about their clothing, which was washed very infrequently – if at all. However, at the end of the day when he retired to bed, the knight would discard all his clothing. Some medieval pictures show us kings in bed wearing their crowns and nothing else.

SIR GAWAIN

For a whole week before New Year's Day the court at Camelot had given itself over to Yuletide feasting and merrymaking. Now the excesses of the last few days had taken their toll, and many of the knights were lolling sleepily in their seats with their belts loosened. As the afternoon grew darker, snores filled the air. Some dogs lay sleeping by the open fire while others scavenged among the bones and other debris from the feasting that littered the rush-strewn floor.

Suddenly there was a mighty rap at the castle doors, and a few moments later the awesome figure of a green knight mounted on a great horse burst into the great hall. The knight was so massively built that he could have been a giant. He was dressed all in green. Even stranger, his hair, hands and even his face were green. The only part of him that was not green were the whites of his eyes, and when he opened his mouth the tongue showed red. The horse, too, was as green as its rider.

'Ha!' bellowed the knight in a voice that quickly roused the dozing knights. 'So this is King Arthur's most noble and renowned company of knights. Nothing but sluggards and drunkards and not one of them, I'll wager, brave enough to stand and fight with me! Well, is that not so, King Arthur?' challenged the knight. He now had the attention of everyone.

'What is your challenge, gentle knight?' asked King Arthur. He hoped that courteous behaviour would soothe this rude and belligerent intruder.

'Ah, mighty king, I do not come to wage war for I am not wearing my armour. But I come with a wager. I say that not one of your knights is brave enough to stand up and strike me with a single blow with this axe on any part of my body I choose. Perhaps one will do this, but will he be prepared to swear to meet me after a year and let me strike a return blow at him?' He brandished the great axe he was carrying and his body shook with a great rumbling laugh which made the dogs whimper and the ladies of the court turn pale.

King Arthur looked round his knights, but not one of them would meet his eye. Dismayed to meet such a lack of response, and angered at the arrogance of this uncouth knight, King Arthur said: 'Dismount and I will meet your challenge.'

No sooner had he said this than Sir Gawain sprang to his feet. Sir Gawain had the reputation among King Arthur's knights of being the most headstrong knight, and he was also much given to exaggeration.

'Sire, do not demean yourself by fighting with this cur. No one shall be better

pleased than I to take a swing at him. Why, I could strike off his insolent head with a single blow.'

Delighted to have a challenger, the Green Knight dismounted. Planting his massive legs squarely on the ground he stood like a colossus. He handed his great axe to Sir Gawain.

'Come nearer, lily-livered knight. Tell me your name. Let me see if your puny arm is as strong as you think it is. Come, strike a blow at my neck. Cut off my head. But mind you take only one blow,' jeered the Green Knight, who stood firm with his hands on his hips, his neck bare ready to receive the blow.

Sir Gawain, now very angry, said, 'I am Sir Gawain.' Then he held the axe firmly in both hands and took a deep breath. The axe swished forward through the air and sliced the Green Knight's head clean from his shoulders.

The court let out an appalled gasp. But as the head fell the Green Knight caught it dexterously before it reached the ground. Defying all belief, he nimbly leapt into his saddle and, holding the severed head by its long green strands of hair, he rode out of the hall with the head crying out these words: 'Meet me in the Chapel of the Green Knight a year from now, Sir Gawain. Then we shall see how *you* withstand *my* blow.'

The year passed quickly. All too soon for Sir Gawain the springtime blossoms had grown and ripened into the fruits of autumn. Now the winter chill crept over the earth, and it was time for Sir Gawain to set off in quest of the chapel where he was honour-bound to meet the Green Knight.

His journey was long and wretched, for as he rode the bitter winter rains poured from the sky and the leafless trees gave him no shelter. As he rode north, snow began to fall. As his weary horse grudgingly picked its way through the heavy fall of snow, Sir Gawain sank lower and lower in the saddle, deeply dejected.

It was soon Christmas Eve and Sir Gawain seemed no nearer his journey's end. His heart grew sad as he thought of the merrymaking that would be taking place at Camelot. Just as his spirits were at their lowest ebb he came to a place where the snow had not fallen. Through the trees he saw the welcoming lights of a fine castle. He rode up to the drawbridge thinking that here he might at least find food and shelter for one night before continuing on his quest.

The castle's drawbridge was down, so Gawain rode across it and into the courtyard. He was warmly welcomed by a group of squires. They took his horse and led him inside, where they gave him a hot bath and a new set of warm clothes. Then the lord of the castle appeared. He was a large, jovial man, full of good cheer. When he discovered that Gawain was a knight of the Round Table on a quest he said: 'Sir, you are welcome here, especially at this festive time of year.'

Sir Gawain's spirits were quickly restored and all the discomforts of his journey were forgotten. He was led into the hall where the table had been newly laid with a clean, white cloth. Silver goblets and plates had been set on the table, and soon mouth-watering food was carried in – capons, pheasants and wild boar. Sir Gawain sat down and enjoyed the best meal he had tasted for many weeks. After supping, his host led him to his private chamber. Seated by the fire, sewing, was the most beautiful woman Sir Gawain had ever seen. His host introduced her as his wife and while the two men talked the lady waited on them, bringing them steaming goblets of hot, spiced wine. By the end of the evening it was agreed that Sir Gawain should stay at this castle for Christmas.

The next three days passed quickly for Sir Gawain, being spent in feasting, dancing, singing and merrymaking. It was one of the happiest Christmases of his life for this knight was a most courteous and attentive host. His wife, too, saw that Sir Gawain lacked for nothing. Sir Gawain had quite forgotten the quest which had led him to this castle. However, on the fourth day he remembered that by New Year's Day he had to find the Chapel of the Green Knight.

'Sir, you have been a most generous host but tomorrow I will have to leave your pleasant castle for I must find the chapel of the Green Knight by New Year's Day. I am afraid that I have not left myself enough time to do this,' said Sir Gawain.

His host laughed: 'Why, there is no need for you to go tomorrow. The chapel you seek is but a couple of hours' ride from this very castle. Stay and enjoy the rest of the Christmas festivities with us. On New Year's Day one of my squires will take you to the chapel.'

'This is the best news I have heard for a long time,' said Sir Gawain, 'for I had sworn on oath to be there on that day. Until now I was afraid that I should fail in this quest.'

'For the next three days I ride from the castle to hunt,' said his host. 'Stay at the castle and rest, for you have had an arduous journey and need to gather your strength before continuing on your quest. My wife shall entertain you while I am gone.' This seemed a good idea to Sir Gawain and he agreed to do this.

Before they retired that evening the lord of the castle said: 'As it is the festive season, it is a good time for laying wagers. I shall give you what I win at hunting if, in return, you give me whatever prize you win in the castle while I am away hunting.' Sir Gawain agreed to this wager. He could not, however, think of any prize he might win at the castle.

Next morning the lord of the castle rode off to hunt long before Sir Gawain was awake. Sir Gawain had slept late in his warm and comfortable bed. He was awakened when the lady of the castle tripped into the chamber shining as brightly as one of the sunbeams which was pouring through the window. She sat on Sir Gawain's bed, chattered gaily with him and before long their conversation turned to love.

'I think it strange that such a courteous knight as you can sit and talk so long with a lady and not ask her for a kiss,' teased his hostess.

Sir Gawain was taken aback and replied: 'Madam, I did not ask for a kiss because a true knight should ask for nothing. He fears that if he did it might displease the lady.

But if you wish I shall ask you for a kiss.' At that, the lady leant forward and kissed him sweetly. Before the astonished Sir Gawain could say anything she had slipped gracefully from the chamber.

That evening the lord of the castle returned in good humour, for it had been a good day's hunting. He presented the spoils of the chase to Sir Gawain: a splendid red deer.

'I have kept my side of the bargain. Now you must give to me whatever prize you won here today,' said the knight.

Sir Gawain could not immediately think what he had won. Then he thought of the kiss he had won from the lady. He went over to the knight and, placing his hands on his shoulders, he planted a kiss on his host's astonished mouth.

The lord of the castle burst out laughing: 'A fine prize to win! I do not think that I shall ask you from whom you won that!' Still laughing, the two men went in to supper.

Next morning the lady of the castle again came and woke Sir Gawain when her lord had gone from the castle to hunt. After they had flirted and talked of love she left Sir Gawain, having kissed him twice. When the lord returned and had presented his prize of a wild boar to Sir Gawain he received two kisses from his guest.

'I should perhaps ask you from whom you gained those kisses,' said his host.

'But that was not part of our bargain,' replied Sir Gawain quickly. Their daily wager settled, the two men went to eat.

On the third morning the lady came to Sir Gawain's room and awoke him with a kiss. When he was sitting up in bed she kissed him again and asked him: 'Why do you not ask me for more than kisses? I begin to think that you are made of ice. Or does your heart belong to a lady at Camelot?'

'I am bound to no lady. But you, madam, you have a lord who is a most noble knight. In all honour and conscience I cannot, and will not, ask for more from you.'

'But he is away all day,' the lady reminded him. 'Tell me, how is he to know what happens when he is not here?'

'By my knighthood,' declared Sir Gawain, 'I shall not be part of such a shameful deed as you suggest.'

'Sir Gawain, you are indeed a noble knight,' replied the lady, 'I shall plague you no further. As you will not love me, have you no gift for me to remember you by?'

'When I left Camelot on this quest I brought nothing with me,' said Sir Gawain.

'Then I shall give you a gift,' said the lady, and she drew from round her slender waist a green and wonderfully embroidered belt.

'But lady,' said Sir Gawain, 'I cannot wear your gift because I am not your knight. In all honour I cannot carry your favour.'

'It is such a little thing,' said the lady. 'You may easily wear it hidden beneath your clothes. Then my husband need not know you wear my favour. Take it, I beg you, for it is a magic belt. When you wear it no blows you receive shall harm you.'

Sir Gawain immediately thought of his ordeal the following day when he would meet the Green Knight. The protection given by the magic belt was too powerful a temptation for him to resist, and he accepted the gift. The lady gave Sir Gawain a third kiss and left the room. Sir Gawain rose from his bed and dressed carefully, wearing the belt beneath his shirt so that no one could see it.

When his host returned to the castle that evening he had but a fox's skin to show for his day's hunting. Sir Gawain gave him the three kisses he had won that day. This done, the two men sat down to supper. Sir Gawain, however, did not tell of the belt he had received from his host's wife.

Sir Gawain slept little that night, for his mind was filled with thoughts of his ordeal on the following day.

Next morning he had no appetite for breakfast. He was helped into his armour and his horse was brought from the stables in to the courtyard. He mounted and bade farewell to his host, who had come down into the cold morning air to say goodbye to his guest.

Sir Gawain rode across the drawbridge followed closely by the squire who was to lead him to the chapel of the Green Knight.

There was no sun that morning and the air was chill and damp as Sir Gawain rode. He had with him the Green Knight's axe. Sadly he thought that this might well be the last morning he should ever see, for the Green Knight's blow would surely slay him. However, he had the magic belt, so perhaps he need not despair yet.

Sir Gawain and the squire rode until they came to a mist-filled valley, where the squire said: 'I dare not come with you any further. In the valley before you is the Green Chapel you seek. People say that the Green Knight who lurks there is the most fearsome warrior. If I were you, I would ride away rather than meet him, for he will surely slay you.'

'I am bound to meet him,' replied Sir Gawain, and, thanking the squire for guiding him to this place, he rode away into the misty valley.

Soon he came to some ruins which could only have been the remains of the chapel but he could not see the Green Knight. Suddenly, from behind a massive boulder, the Green Knight appeared. He looked as fearsome as when he had first ridden into the hall at Camelot. However, his head was once again firmly on his shoulders.

'You have come on the appointed day, Sir Gawain,' said the Green Knight in his rumbling voice. 'Give me my axe and prepare to receive my blow.'

Sir Gawain gave him the axe and dismounted. While the Green Knight began to

sharpen the blade on a rock, a paralyzing shiver ran up Sir Gawain's spine. He somehow managed to remove his helmet. Then he knelt, his neck bared, ready to receive the blow.

He closed his eyes and heard the Green Knight walk towards him and stop. A few seconds later he felt a rush of air pass by his neck but the blade did not touch him. He was at a loss, for surely no one could have missed such an easy target. Once again he steeled himself for the blow. A second time the blade glanced by his neck but did not touch him. He lifted his head and saw the Green Knight raise the axe and, for a third time swing a blow at his head. This time the blade struck his neck. The cut stung and Sir Gawain could feel the warm blood trickling down his neck. He put his hand to the wound. Now, he thought, we can fight in equal combat, for I have received his blow, and he reached for his sword. Before he could rise to his feet the Green Knight spoke: 'You withstood the blow well, Sir Gawain. Put down your sword, for I will not strike you again.'

The Green Knight's voice seemed strangely changed, yet it was familiar. Looking up at him, Sir Gawain saw that the Green Knight was none other than the lord of the castle where he had stayed over Christmas. But then he seemed to be the Green Knight again.

'How did this come about?' asked the bemused Sir Gawain. 'And why did you strike three blows at me?'

'The magic that causes this transformation is not for you to understand, Sir Gawain. As to your other question, I stopped short on two blows because twice you

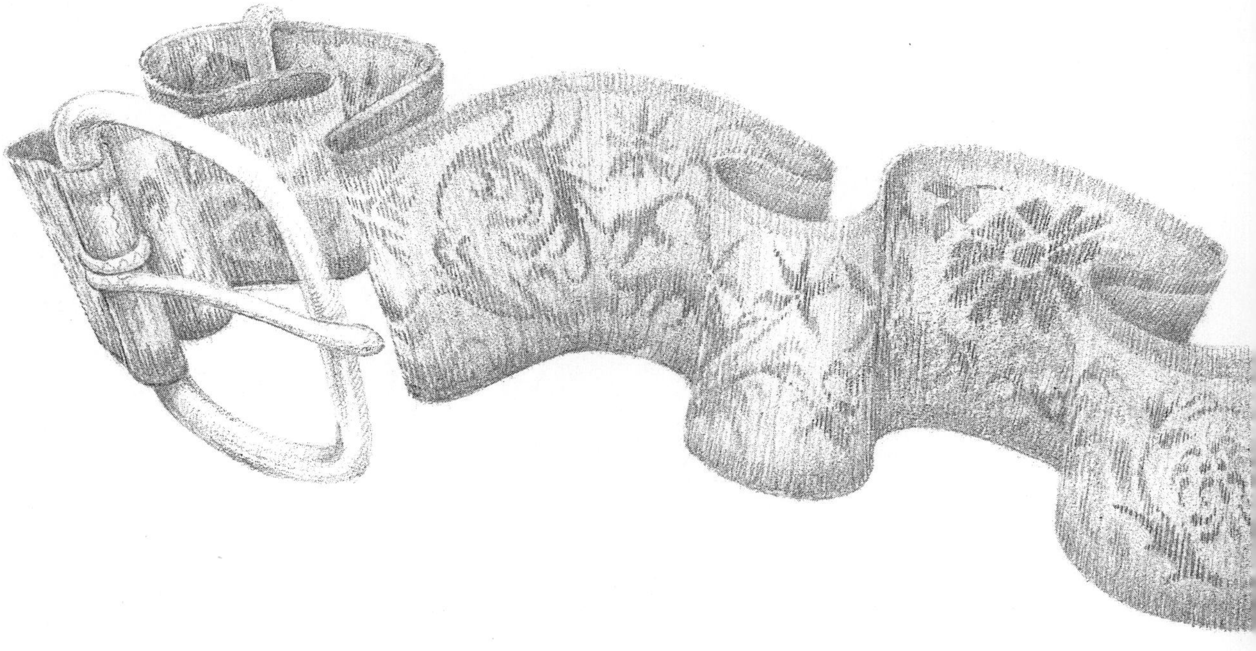

told me the truth of the prizes you gained in my castle while I was hunting. But I cut you with the third blow for while you told me of one prize you hid from me the belt my wife gave you. If you had taken more from my wife I would not have hesitated to cut your head from your shoulders.'

Sir Gawain was now bitterly ashamed of his behaviour. In accepting the belt, and failing to confess the gift as agreed, he had not acted as an honourable knight. However, his host comforted him, assuring him that few men would have contented themselves with mere kisses from his beautiful wife.

The two knights rode back towards the castle. The knight told him his name was Sir Bernlak and that he had wished to see for himself whether the honourable reputation of the Knights of the Round Table was genuine.

'I instructed my wife to tempt you, Sir Gawain. You only took her belt because you wished to protect your life,' said Sir Bernlak.

'Yes, but that still makes me a coward,' moaned Sir Gawain. 'I am not worthy to sit at the Round Table. I am dishonoured and would rather you had cut off my head.'

'Take heart, you are but a young knight with much to learn,' said Sir Bernlak, consolingly. 'But you were courageous enough to keep your oath and journey to find me to endure my blow. That in itself has proved to me that King Arthur's knights are truly the bravest and most dutiful of men.'

The men parted on good terms and Sir Gawain rode back to Camelot to relate the outcome of his adventure.

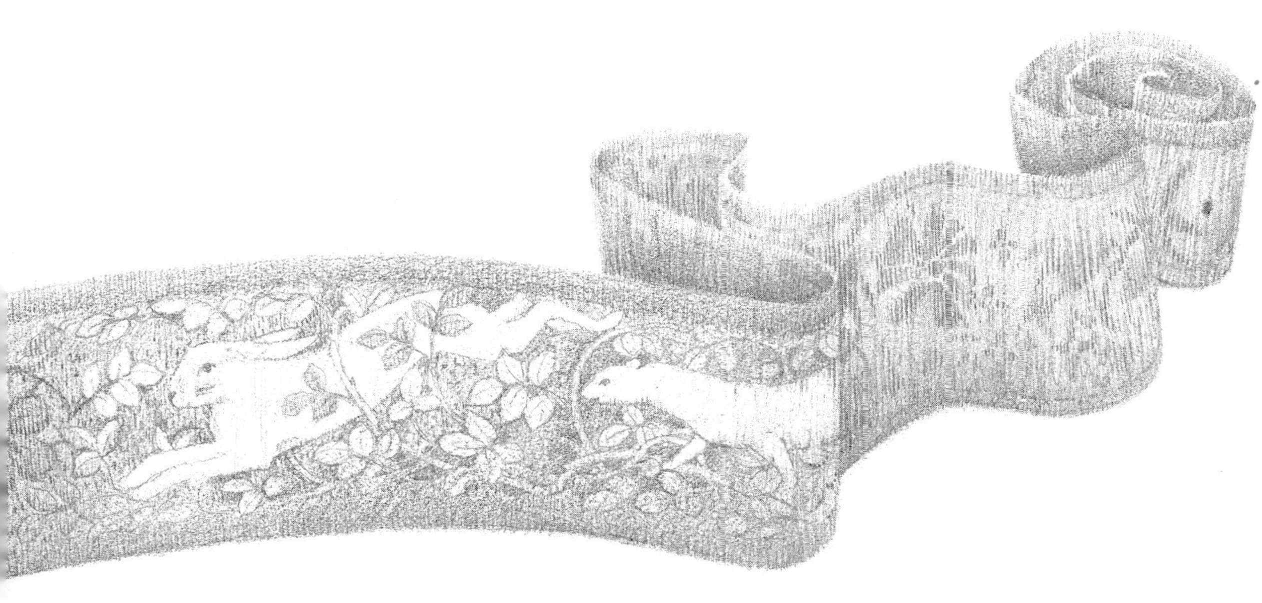

FEASTING

'A man who eats well will never be a coward' said a knight when asked by a Saracen what gave the crusading knights their great strength. Eating and drinking well were among the great pleasures of the knight's life. Rising at six in the morning, he would eat only a modest breakfast because the main meal of the day, made up of several courses of meat or fowl, began about 10 am.

Each knight sought to outdo his peers in the lavishness of his table. This, he believed, showed to advantage his knightly quality of generosity, or *largesse.* To this end one knight, in a show of culpable extravagance, had a meal for 300 guests cooked over candles, a most expensive commodity in the medieval world.

Feasts could consist of up to fifteen courses and would often last eight hours or more. A feast was, in fact, the ideal way to pass a winter's day. Set apart from the rest of the company, knights would sit at a trestle table covered with a white cloth. One of the many duties of squires was to learn to lay this high table correctly. The salt cellar, often in the shape of a silver ship, formed an important decoration on the top table. (At this time salt was not added in the preparation of food.) To 'sit below the salt' therefore meant not to be among the most important people. Another table decoration was the aquamanile, a bronze vessel which held perfumed water in which the diners could wash their hands. These aquamaniles were either in the shape of a knight, mounted on a horse, or a monster. Knights were most scrupulous about washing their hands before eating.

The dishes brought in might include a boar's head, whole

suckling pigs, fish, venison and other game, and perhaps roast peacock. At one splendid feast a peacock was served which had been carefully skinned to keep all the feathers and skin intact. It was then roasted and the skin replaced, with the tail feathers fanned out so that the bird looked lifelike. A piece of wool rubbed with camphor was placed in the bird's mouth. Once at the table this was lit, and the bird instantly spewed out flames like a little volcano. Some knights even covered peacocks in gold leaf for the table.

Another *pièce de resistance* was a pie out of which, when the crust was broken, would fly bewildered little birds. Sadly, the knight would then allow his falcons to demolish these birds.

Root vegetables were not eaten by knights, who considered these foods suitable only for peasants.

Some of the dishes would be highly spiced to encourage the knights to drink more wine. Knights drank only wine and would not touch water – a sensible precaution as this could well have been contaminated.

Knights had no forks, of course, as these are a comparatively recent invention. They used spoons, knives and fingers, and ate from wooden plates, or trenchers. These were originally made of bread and could be eaten after the meal. To clear the plate before the next course the diner would either wipe the trencher with bread or lick it clean. There was always plenty of water on the table for rinsing greasy fingers, but as there were no towels the knight would simply wipe his fingers on the table-cloth.

As the feast progressed diners were permitted to loosen their belts while watching the antics of jugglers and acrobats.

FALCONRY

Knights took the greatest pride in their falcons for they were a sign of high social standing. They took the birds with them everywhere – out riding, into the castle and even into church. Some became so attached to their birds that they would make pilgrimages to holy shrines in order to pray for the recovery of a sick bird.

The main sport in falconry was to teach the bird to rise from its owner's wrist at command, swoop down on and kill its prey, then wait until the hunter's hound retrieved the prey before returning to the owner's wrist.

Known as 'birds of the fist', falcons were carried on tough leather gloves. This gauntlet was often very ornately decorated, and probably bore the knight's heraldic device. The bird's head was covered with a tiny leather hood or *chapel* which left the bird's nostrils and mouth free to breathe. Tiny bells or *campanelles* were attached to its leg by a soft leather thong or jess.

The knight had to ride with the bird on his right arm, held at 90 degrees from the elbow. His arm had to be steady and the bird's face had to face the direction of the wind. For safety, and to avoid alarming the bird, it would be held as far from the man's face as possible. A knight who drank too much could not have made a good falconer as he would not have been able to keep his arm steady.

Great skill and patience were involved in training falcons. They were usually trained in an open meadow where they were taught to rise from the owner's wrist on command. A string was attached to one of the bird's claws and when the bird had circled round it would be reeled in at the falconer's command. Birds often broke loose. As a page, Thomas à Becket (later Henry II's Archbishop of Canterbury) nearly lost his life when chasing an errant falcon because when he dived into a turbulent millchase to rescue the bird he was almost drowned.

Housed in buildings called mews and resting on wooden perches called *sedilles,* falcons were well fed – on the flesh of other fowl. If the flesh was warm from the killing so much the better, but otherwise it would be heated. If no fowl was available then the bird might be given unsalted cheese or scrambled eggs.

If a falcon was stolen, or if, after escaping, it was found and kept by its finder, the penalty was severe: the falcon was allowed to eat six ounces of flesh from the culprit's breast.

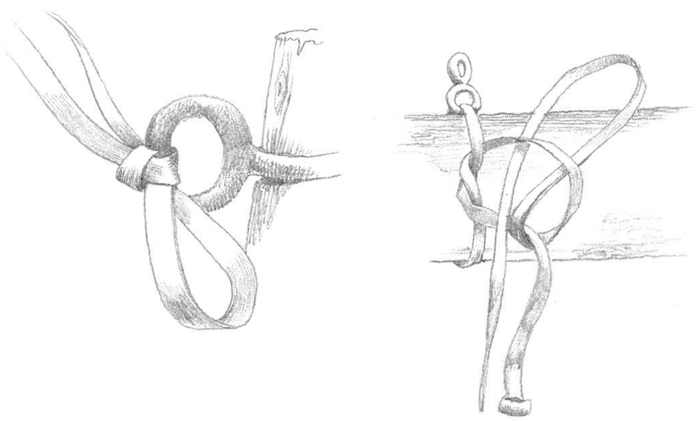

One of the main responsibilities of the falconer was to ensure the security of his birds. The leash was attached to the perch by a simple, yet secure, knot. Some perches were set high, at a man's eye-level. The **sedille,** however, was made from a conical block of wood set on the ground. This had a ring in the side to which the leash was attached. The falconer would remove the bird from its perch to take it out for air early in the morning.

The campanelle and **swivel** (often made of two links of mail) were shackled to the bird's foot with the **jess.** The **leash** to keep the bird on his perch was then attached to the swivel.

SIR GARETH

One Whitsuntide when King Arthur and his knights were gathered at Camelot a young man entered the great hall. Although he was dressed in shabby clothes, his large hands and broad shoulders indicated that this was someone who must surely have been trained to wield a sword and hold a lance.

The stranger was unabashed by the noble company facing him. Striding over to where King Arthur was seated, he bent down on one knee and said: 'Sire, I have heard that at your court any man who proves his worth may become a knight. Grant me three favours and I shall show myself as worthy of knighthood as any of your knights here.'

Arthur was amazed, yet amused, by the young man's self-assurance. 'Ask what you wish,' he said.

'Give me food and lodging at Camelot for twelve months,' he said. 'This done, I will then make my second request.'

'Why, this is an easy favour to grant,' said King Arthur. 'But first, tell me your name.'

'Sire, I cannot do that,' replied the stranger. 'But trust me when I say that I have as much right as any man to be here at Camelot.'

King Arthur respected the young man's wish and instructed his steward, Sir Kay, to see that the stranger was given board and lodging. The haughty Sir Kay, however, thought it impertinent of this country boy to presume that he could keep company with knights. But Sir Kay did as he was commanded. However, he set the stranger to work in the kitchens, making sure that he was given only the most menial of tasks. It soon became evident that the youth had never worked in a kitchen: he burnt the roasts, dropped the eggs and generally showed no domestic accomplishment.

Sir Kay taunted him continually and scornfully called him 'Beaumains', or 'he with the beautiful hands', because his large, white hands were quite unused to plucking game, scrubbing floors or turning the spit.

'Beaumains', as he soon became known, endured Sir Kay's insults with a good grace. When other knights saw his great self-control in the face of this treatment they encouraged him to bide his time, for if he could survive this he would surely prove himself worthy to be a knight. Sir Lancelot and Sir Gawain were especially civil to the boy, always ready with a kind word or a few coins.

The twelve months soon passed and once again all the knights were assembled when a damsel on a palfrey rode into the hall.

'King Arthur, I beg for aid. My sister, the Lady of Lyonesse, is being besieged in her castle by the fearsome Red Knight,' cried the damsel. 'I entreat you, let one of your knights come with me to free her.'

'Who shall follow this adventure?' asked the king. Before anyone could answer Beaumains had rushed forward.

'Sire, grant me my second favour and let me go on this quest.'

All were astonished at his boldness, but still Beaumains continued his plea: 'If this request is granted, let me also ask my third favour: let Sir Lancelot follow me, and if my actions show I am worthy to be a knight let him dub me. I wish above all else to receive this honour from no man but he.' So fervent were the kitchen boy's entreaties that Arthur told him that the quest should be his. Immediately, Arthur wondered if he had made the right decision, but he had a strange feeling that he recognized something in Beaumains.

However, he had no time to reflect on this, for the damsel, whose name was Linnet, was furiously asking, 'Is this how you regard my sister, besieged in the Castle Dangerous? Can you send her nothing better than a kitchen boy for a champion?'

Remounting her horse, Linnet rode quickly out of the castle. Beaumains immediately ran after her.

'Wait for me,' he cried. 'Wait at least until I have a horse and sword.'

Beaumains was soon out of sight in frantic pursuit of Linnet.

Sir Kay was incensed at this turn of events. He despatched Dragonet, the king's fool, mounted on a donkey, dressed in armour that had seen better days and armed with a blunt sword, to bring back his errant kitchen boy. However, when Dragonet caught up with Beaumains the kitchen boy quickly knocked Dragonet from his donkey and took his sword.

'Forgive me, Dragonet,' said Beaumains, for the fool had been a friend to him, 'but I have greater need than you for this donkey and sword.'

Digging his heels into the donkey's side, he urged the reluctant beast forward. And so Beaumains bounced off into the forest in search of Linnet.

When Dragonet limped back to the castle Sir Kay rode out to bring back his kitchen boy. Sir Lancelot followed him anxious to see that no harm befell Beaumains.

Soon Sir Kay on his strong horse had caught up with Beaumains.

'Come back to the kitchen with me, you miserable boy,' he bellowed.

'I shall not,' said Beaumains, 'for I must accomplish this quest.'

Enraged at Beaumains' impudence, Sir Kay rode at him, intending to drag him from his donkey. Immediately Beaumains drew his blunt sword and attacked Sir Kay. Whether because of his anger at Sir Kay's maltreatment of him or because he was determined not to return to Camelot before he had carried out his quest, Beaumains fought with the strength of ten men. He soon knocked Sir Kay from his horse, and the knight fell unconscious to the ground.

Then Sir Lancelot, smiling, emerged from the nearby trees from where he had watched the fight.

'Is this how they teach you to fight in the kitchens?' he asked.

'No,' said Beaumains. 'I learnt to fight on the island of Orkney, where I was certainly no kitchen boy. I am Gareth, youngest son of King Lot. I think I fight as well as my eldest brother Sir Gawain. You see, I had to prove that I am worthy to be a knight on my own account rather than because I am the youngest brother of one of King Arthur's bravest knights. Knight me, Sir Lancelot, so that I may be a worthy champion of the Lady of Lyonesse,' begged Gareth.

After hearing this story, Sir Lancelot did not hesitate to dub the boy a knight. He

also promised not to reveal his identity to any man. Gareth was now impatient to continue on his quest, so taking Sir Kay's horse and sword as his just prize he rode off through the trees to catch up with Linnet.

'Away with you, you low-born kitchen boy,' said the scornful Linnet when Gareth drew alongside her. 'Return to the smoke and stench of the kitchen where you belong.'

Gareth paid no attention to her and continued to ride beside her. They had not ridden far when they saw a black shield hanging on a dead thorn tree. As they looked at it, the figure of a knight could be seen approaching through the trees. He was dressed in a suit of armour that was as black as a raven.

'Is this King Arthur's champion?' asked the Black Knight.

'No, this is the king's kitchen boy!' said Linnet.

'He has a fine horse for a domestic servant. I think I shall take it from him,' said the arrogant knight.

'Sir Knight, you make very free with my horse,' said Gareth, defiantly. 'If you want it you must first slay me.'

With a malicious laugh the Black Knight rode confidently at Gareth brandishing his sword. Gareth quickly drew his newly-won sword and in an instant the forest rang with the sound of clashing metal. Gareth held his own against his powerful adversary until, with a well-placed thrust, he wounded the Black Knight just where his armour left his neck unprotected. The Black Knight slithered gracelessly from his horse and lay dead on the ground.

Linnet, who had grown pale during the fight, now regained her composure and rode off into the forest without a word to Gareth. With a shrug of his shoulders, Gareth lingered only to take for himself the Black Knight's armour. Then he set out again in pursuit of Linnet.

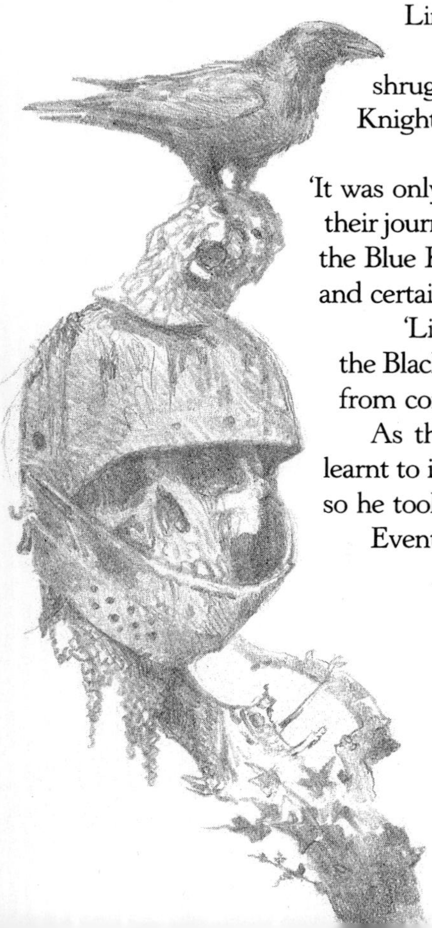

'It was only luck that you slew the Black Knight,' said Linnet as they continued their journey through the forest. 'Soon we shall have to pass through the lands of the Blue Knight. He is one knight you shall not defeat. Some say he is a giant, and certainly no man has yet managed to defeat him.'

'Linnet, you are more than ungracious to give me no credit for defeating the Black Knight in fair combat. But I warn you, nothing you say can deter me from continuing this adventure,' replied Gareth.

As they rode onwards, Linnet continued to belittle Gareth. But he had learnt to ignore all provocation while working in the kitchens of Arthur's court, so he took no notice of her jibes.

Eventually they drew near the edge of the forest, and as they came out of the

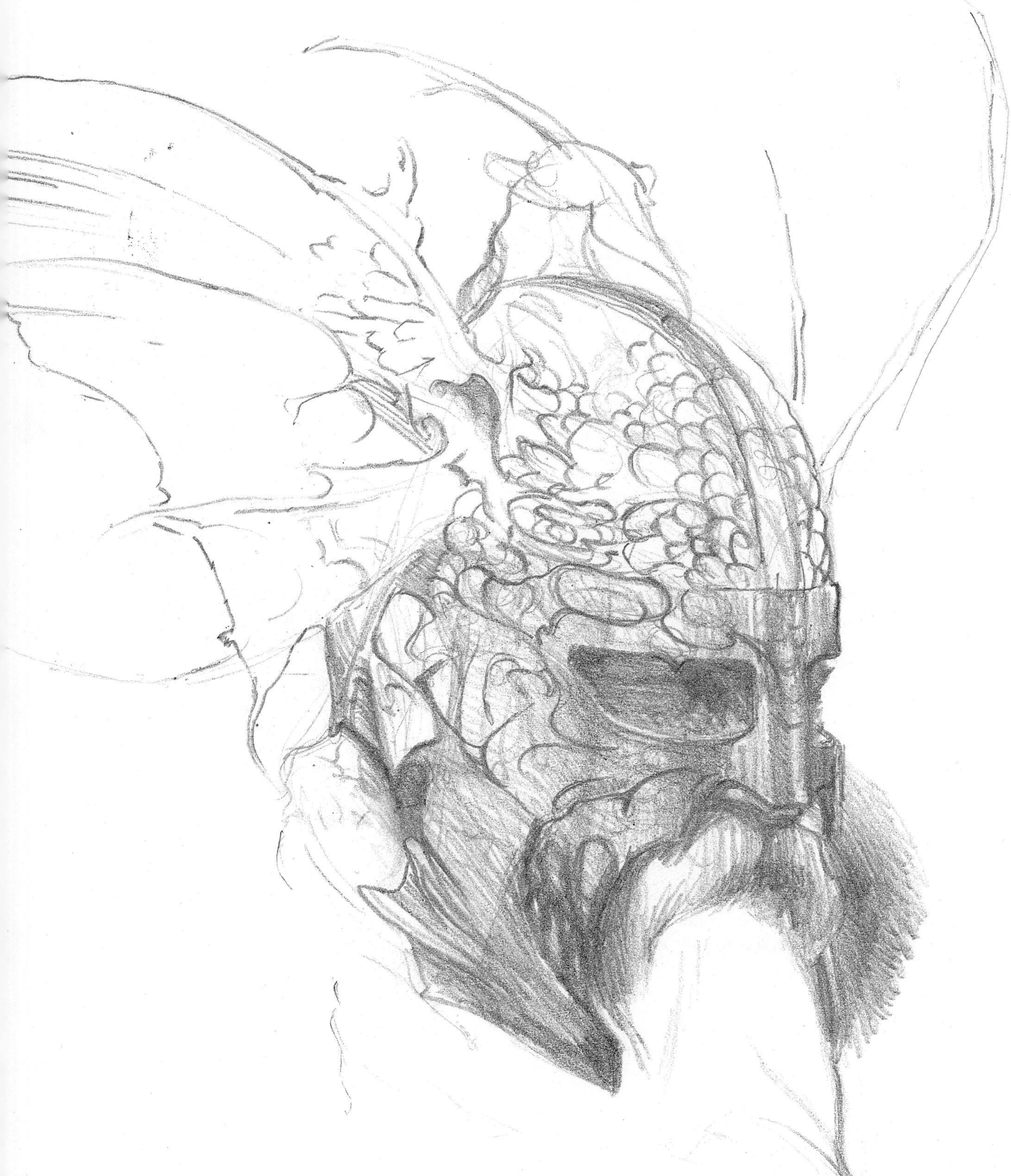

trees they saw before them, pitched in a meadow on the opposite bank of a running stream, a shining, silken blue pavilion.

'Run away while you still have a chance,' said Linnet, 'for this is the Blue Knight's pavilion and, as I told you, no man has ever overcome him.'

'Then I shall be the first,' retorted Gareth. Dismounting from his horse, he walked to a nearby tree on which hung a blue horn and blew a single note summoning the Blue Knight to prepare to meet his challenger.

But Gareth felt a chill run down his back when he saw the Blue Knight emerging from his pavilion. He had never seen such a powerful, menacing figure. He could not see the Blue Knight's face, however, for it was hidden by a helmet of gold. As the Blue Knight strode forward the very ground seemed to shake. The Blue Knight wasted no time on words but straight away drew his sword. By now he had reached the stream on the other side of which stood Gareth, ready to fight.

The two knights advanced, meeting in the middle of the stream. The water was no impediment to the combat. They slashed and hacked at each other, their swords raising clouds of spray which fell upon their armour. The water soon ran red with the blood that flowed from each knight's wounds. Gareth fought with all the strength he could muster but nothing seemed to weaken the Blue Knight. Finally, with one last tremendous effort, he butted his full weight straight at the Blue Knight. The giant was struck off balance and, tottering under the weight of his armour, fell down with a massive splash into the stream. He would have drowned had not Gareth quickly unlaced his helmet.

'Mercy,' begged the Blue Knight as Gareth placed the tip of his sword at his adversary's throat.

'I shall spare you only if the lady wishes it,' said Gareth.

Linnet, who had hardly dared to watch the contest, now ventured forward with a look of sheer amazement on her face. Yet with her usual condescension she said: 'Spare him. It is a pity that so valiant a knight should fall at the hands of a kitchen boy.'

However, the defeated Blue Knight proved to be a most courteous man, and he chided Linnet for her ungracious behaviour towards Gareth. He invited them both to his pavilion, where Linnet tended their wounds. As they ate supper that evening, Gareth told the Blue Knight how he sought to fight the Red Knight.

'He is a terrible foe to seek,' said the Blue Knight. 'But he can be overcome. By some witchcraft beyond my understanding his strength is said to diminish as the sun sets. If you fight him then you may well defeat him.'

Gareth was delighted with this advice and the next morning both Linnet and he parted on good terms with the Blue Knight. Once more they entered the great forest and rode for many hours. As the day was drawing on they came upon a sight which caused the colour to drain from Gareth's cheeks. Hanging in front of them from the bare branches of a tree were the fully-armoured bodies and shields of at least forty knights. These, victims of the Red Knight, were brave men who had failed in their attempts to rescue the Lady of Lyonesse.

On a tree nearby hung an ivory horn. Gareth blew it to summon the Red Knight. In an instant the Red Knight emerged from his red pavilion, pitched beneath the castle walls. Gareth felt his stomach knot in terror at the thought of the contest that was about to begin. Then he glanced towards the castle battlements and caught sight of the beautiful woman for whose sake he was fighting: when the blast of the horn had been heard, everyone knew that another brave knight was about to risk his life to save her.

The sight of the Lady of Lyonesse gave Gareth new heart and he spurred his horse forward to meet the Red Knight.

The two men's horses met with a resounding clash. The impact was such that the girths of their horses' saddles broke. Both men were hurled to the ground and the Red Knight's helmet was dashed from his head. For several minutes both men lay motionless and it seemed that their necks must be broken. Then they staggered to their feet and drew closer to each other, swords at the ready.

They fought long and hard beneath the castle walls. In the heat of the combat each man dropped his sword and picked up that of his opponent to continue the fight. For an hour longer they fought, neither man yielding or staying to draw breath.

The sun sank lower in the sky, and long shadows were cast down from the castle walls. Now Gareth began to fear that he had not the strength to continue. He prayed that what the Blue Knight had told him of his adversary's loss of strength at sundown was true.

'Look up at the castle,' cried Linnet. 'My sister looks towards you.'

Gareth glanced to where the Lady of Lyonesse stood and straight away found new strength. Soon he felt himself weakening again.

Once more Linnet encouraged him: 'Look towards the castle, for my sister weeps to see her champion tire.'

Again Gareth looked quickly towards the battlements and glimpsed, silhouetted against the reddening sky, the beautiful lady whom he must save. Drawing on his last ounce of strength, he drew back his sword and, holding it in both hands, struck the Red Knight a blow which brought him to the ground.

Once down, the Red Knight made no attempt to move. 'Spare me,' he cried, for suddenly he had lost his strength.

'Why should I spare you when you have slain so many worthy knights and terrorized this lady?' asked Gareth.

'It was witchcraft that did this,' said the Red Knight. 'The brother of the lady I loved was killed by one of King Arthur's knights, and for love of her I swore vengeance on all knights from his kingdom. When this was discovered by an enchantress who wished evil on King Arthur I became her unwilling victim. Her magic, which is powerful only during the hours of daylight, is what gave me my superhuman strength. But now, by your conquest, the spell is broken.'

Gareth spared the Red Knight, for he judged that he was not totally responsible for his deeds. But he made the Red Knight swear that from that moment he would serve King Arthur and fight only for him.

Gareth now made his way to the castle where the lady joyfully welcomed her rescuer. Under the Lady of Lyonesse's gentle care Gareth quickly recovered from his wounds and during this time the couple fell in love. But Gareth, with his usual pride, would not marry her until he had won further glory. Although it grieved him, he left her castle in search of new adventures and for many months there was neither sight nor sound of him.

Meanwhile at Camelot, Gareth's mother, the Queen of Orkney, had arrived to see how her youngest son was faring. Then it was revealed that Beaumains was none other than Gareth, Sir Gawain's youngest brother. For Sir Lancelot, true to his promise, had not revealed Gareth's identity. Distressed that he had not recognized his brother, Gawain immediately set out to find Gareth. His journey soon led him to the Castle Dangerous. There the Lady of Lyonesse sadly told him that she did not know where Gareth was.

Now the Lady of Lyonesse was naturally anxious to see Gareth again. Turning her mind to the problem, she soon had an idea. She decided to hold a tournament at her castle, offering as the victor's prize her hand in marriage.

Messengers were despatched throughout the land to proclaim the tournament. The Lady of Lyonesse felt sure that such an event, and such a prize, would draw Gareth from wherever his travels had taken him.

Soon the day of the tournament arrived. For many days all the forest paths leading to the castle had been decked with garlands of flowers to show the way to the event. So great an occasion was expected that King Arthur and his court had travelled to the castle to enjoy the spectacle.

Early in the morning the heralds walked to the lists and proclaimed the start of the tournament. A dazzling sight in their most elaborate armour, mounted on horses bedecked with colourful caparisons, the knights divided into two teams for the melée. Soon the opposing sides were fighting hell for leather, taking prisoners and knocking opponents from their horses. After a while most of the knights had withdrawn, injured or overcome, from the field. But still there was no sign of Gareth. It seemed that Sir Gawain would be declared victor, for he was still mounted and fighting. The Lady of Lyonesse looked in vain for Gareth.

Then a cloud of dust was seen in the distance and a knight resplendent in white armour inlaid with gold approached at a gallop. He rode straight into the tournament area and engaged Sir Gawain in combat.

The two knights fought fiercely until Linnet cried out from her stand: 'Sir Gawain, do not fight your brother!'

She had recognized Gareth by the way he used his sword.

The knights immediately stopped fighting and removed their helmets. Amidst great rejoicing, Gareth was reunited first with his brother then with the Lady of Lyonesse, and the happy couple decided to marry without delay.

Linnet, however, regretted for the rest of her life that the kitchen boy to whom she had behaved so ungraciously should have proved to be a prince and a most valiant knight.

THE TOURNAMENT

The tournament, or mock battle, was the knights' favourite recreation. When the English king Henry II outlawed tournaments as being too dangerous, his two sons overcame the ban by travelling to the continent in pursuit of this sport.

Tournaments enabled knights to enhance their reputations as warriors and also to keep in good fighting trim in case of a real war. They could increase their fortunes, too, because prisoners taken in a tournament were held for ransom. Poor knights often made their fortunes in this way, and one knight, William Marshall, won ransoms from 103 knights he had captured over a period of ten months.

However, there was always a risk of sustaining serious injury by taking part in a tournament, and eventually strict rules of conduct were laid down: blunted weapons had to be used; no blows could be struck from behind, nor could one strike one's opponent if he had lost his helmet; to aim a blow too low or too high could be considered treasonable; and if any knight hit another man's horse he was disqualified. (Horses were well-protected: the colourful panoplies they wore hid a whole structure of defensive armour.) Social qualifications also came into play: no knight could participate unless he had proved noble descent from four grandparents. Robber knights and any knight who had been a usurer were excluded from tournaments.

In the joust, as opposed to the melée (a free-for-all in which the knights divided into two teams and fought each other), the contest between two knights followed a set sequence. First came the encounter with the lance; the combatants galloped, or rather lumbered, down the lists towards each other (it was difficult to

go fast because of the heavy defensive armour worn by both knight and horse); lances were lowered, heads drawn well down for the moment of impact, and each man aimed to hit his opponent square on the shield, thereby unhorsing him. Often a knight would completely miss his target, but if his lance was broken his squire would rush forward with a replacement.

When three lances had been broken, swords were drawn. If no victor emerged the knights would dismount and continue to fight on foot, each using his heavy suit of armour to buffet his opponent in an attempt to throw him off balance. The first man to fall to the ground, either from wounds or from a blow that proved the greater strength of his adversary, would yield and ask for mercy.

Unfortunately not all jousts were chivalrous affairs. They were often the excuse for settling old feuds. Despite the rules, it was not difficult to substitute a sharp rather than a blunted sword. Nor was the usual prize for the victor the hand of a beautiful damsel: more often than not it was a jewel or a piece of armour.

However, the occasion was not entirely lacking in romance. Knights always sought to wear the colours of a lady. At one tournament the ladies who had a champion taking part led their knights to the lists before the tournament by golden chains. On other occasions knights assumed the names of such heroes as Lancelot or Gawain, hoping that their identification with these legendary knights would bring success to their endeavours.

At the end of the tournament – for all but the wounded – there was feasting, singing and dancing, arranged by the tournament host. Here the knights relaxed and agreed their ransoms.

WEAPONS

Although the sword was the knight's chief weapon, he was also expert in using other weapons such as the lance, battle-axe, mace, club and dagger.

The lance could only be used by a knight, and after the sword it was his chief offensive weapon. However, whereas the sword lasted for a lifetime the lance was highly expendable – one knight boasted of splintering 300 lances in a single tournament. It took great skill to wield a lance, for it was at least 8 feet long, and had to be held steady when riding towards one's opponent if one was to find one's target. Pages would learn how to use a lance at an early age.

In the melée of a tournament or the midst of a battle where there was no room to wield a sword, the battle-axe was used. Its

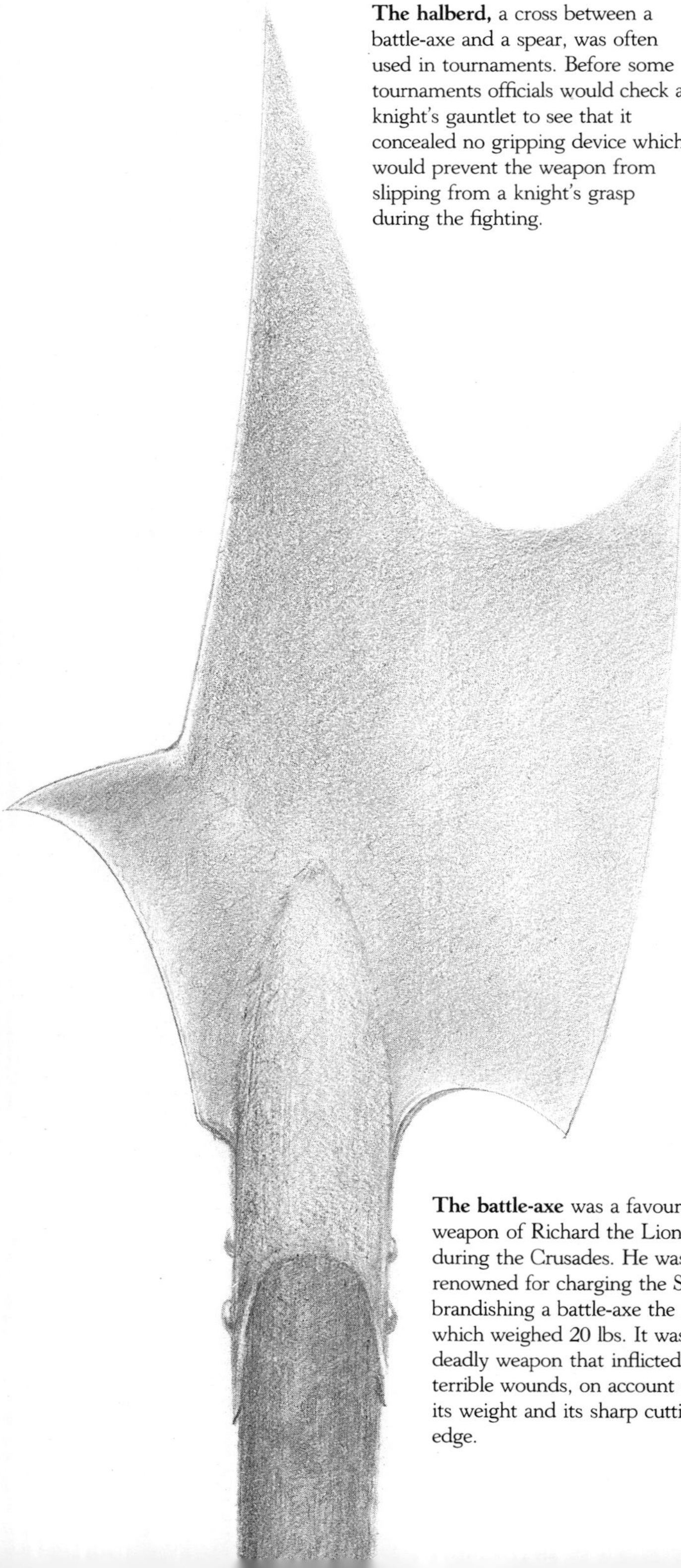

The halberd, a cross between a battle-axe and a spear, was often used in tournaments. Before some tournaments officials would check a knight's gauntlet to see that it concealed no gripping device which would prevent the weapon from slipping from a knight's grasp during the fighting.

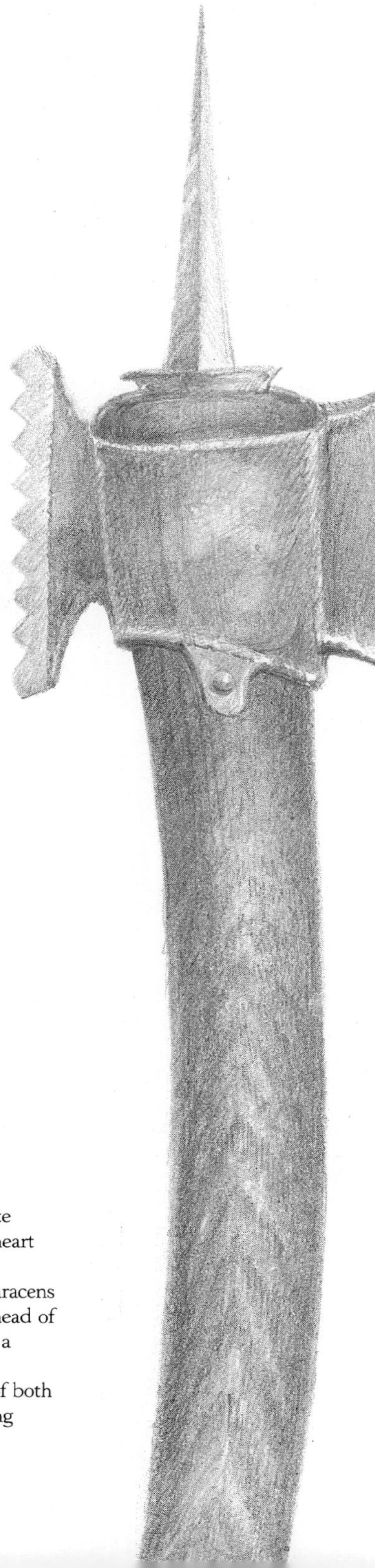

The battle-axe was a favourite weapon of Richard the Lionheart during the Crusades. He was renowned for charging the Saracens brandishing a battle-axe the head of which weighed 20 lbs. It was a deadly weapon that inflicted terrible wounds, on account of both its weight and its sharp cutting edge.

To prevent serious injury in a joust it was common practice for participants to cover the sharpened tip of the lance head with a special **coronal,** or button, to make the weapon blunt. The tournament, however, still remained for many, especially the clergy, 'an execrable and accursed game'.

weight and the sharpness of the axe's cutting edge meant it could inflict terrible wounds. No wonder it was often known as 'the bonecrusher'.

Maces and clubs were primitive wooden weapons made more fearsome by the addition of metal spikes. They were often used by priests who took part in battles. The gospels forbade priests to use a sword or shed blood, and so, following the letter rather than the spirit of the law, they wielded maces instead. Ironically, the mace survives today as a sanctified ceremonial relic carried at the head of solemn processions.

Finally, the knight would always carry a dagger, which looked very much like a small sword but with a longer and thinner blade. The dagger was worn on the right side, the sword being worn on the left.

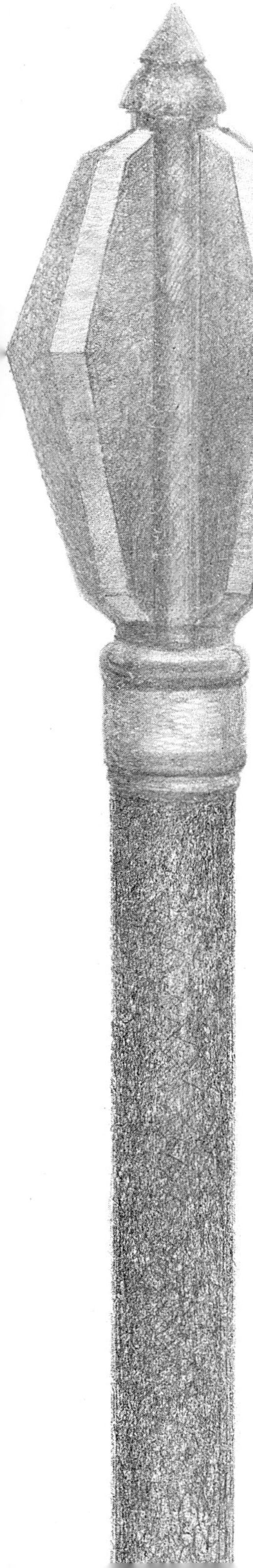

A mace made of wood with a quatrefoil-shaped head. It was carried slung by a loop on the right wrist so that, if sword or lance were lost in combat, the mace could be used at once.

The morning star was guaranteed to make the recipient of a blow see stars. A type of mace, it was made of a wooden ball studded with sharp spikes and attached to a wooden handle by a chain.

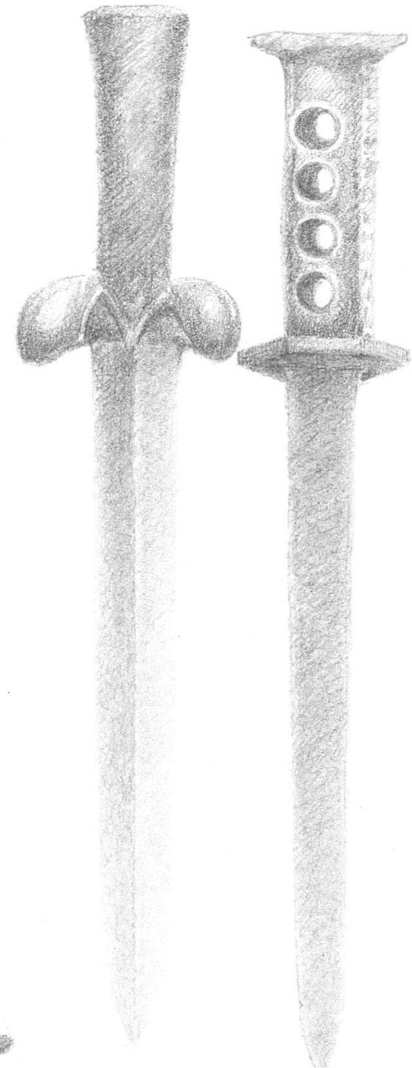

The dagger, otherwise known as the *misericorde* or the dagger of mercy, was used to deliver the death blow to a fallen knight.

SIR TRISTRAM

One hot summer's afternoon Queen Guinevere with a band of knights and ladies was resting in a shady green meadow below Camelot when the sweet sound of a harp was heard. It came from the nearby forest and soon the assembled company saw a man emerge from the trees. As he walked, lost in a world of his own, his fingers continued to pluck out the same haunting melody on his harp.

'Minstrel, it must be a lucky lady for whom that tune was made,' said the queen when the man had reached the place where the party was seated. 'Is there a tale you can tell us to match this tune?'

'There is, madam,' said the minstrel with a deep sigh and, setting his harp on the ground, he sat down and began his story.

I tell you the tale of Tristram, a Prince of Lyonesse. While out hunting one day his father, King Melodias, was taken prisoner by four enchantresses. When his wife, Queen Elizabeth, who was expecting their child, rushed to the forest to try to find him the shock caused her to give birth prematurely. At once the queen knew that this birth would be the death of her and looking at her new-born son, she told her maids, 'Let my son be called Tristram, meaning "of sorrowful birth", for I fear that his coming into the world has killed his mother.'

When King Melodias escaped from the enchantresses he was grief-stricken and he could not bear to look at his infant son. The baby was entrusted to the care of a kindly old man named Gouvernail. He loved Tristram like a son, and in his care Tristram grew strong and brave. Gouvernail also took Tristram with him on his travels to many lands. The happiest time Tristram spent was in France, where he learnt to play the harp. So skilled a harpist did he become that no one in the whole world could match his playing.

Time had lessened King Melodias' grief at his wife's death and Tristram, now a young man, was able to return to his father's court. But he soon grew impatient with court life. He longed to go out into the world in search of adventure. Day by day he grew more restless. Then a traveller arrived from the court of Tristram's uncle, King Mark of Cornwall.

This man told how King Anguish of Ireland was demanding tribute from King Mark. Many years ago the Cornish King had waged war on King Anguish and had been defeated. King Mark had never paid the tribute owing to the Irish king and this

same king had now sent his champion to Cornwall to demand payment: either the kings' champions should settle the matter through single combat, or thirty Cornish youths of noble blood must be sent as slaves to the Irish king. It appeared that so fearsome was the reputation of the Irish champion, Sir Marhaus, that no Cornish knight dared to fight him.

Tristram had been waiting for just such an opportunity. However, as he had not been knighted he did not see how he could be his uncle's champion. 'Why shouldn't my uncle, King Mark, knight me?' he thought. No sooner had this occurred to him than he set off to Cornwall.

When he reached the court, he was enraged to see what a timorous group of knights served King Mark: not one of them had the courage to fight the Irish champion, Sir Marhaus. King Mark himself was in despair, for being unable to find a champion he feared that he would have to pay the tribute demanded by King Anguish.

'Knight me, uncle, and I shall fight for you,' pleaded Tristram. So insistent was his entreaty that although King Mark feared his nephew was no match for the Irish champion, he finally relented and dubbed Tristram a knight. King Mark furnished Tristram with a fine suit of armour and gave him a sword as befitted his champion. Straight away Tristram sent a messenger to the ship where Sir Marhaus was waiting for a challenger.

It was arranged that the champions should meet on a small island which lay in the

bay below the cliffs on which stood Tintagel Castle in Cornwall. Sir Marhaus demanded that there should be no other man on this island save the two knights.

Tristram did not suspect for a moment that this condition could mean treachery. He left the Cornish court amidst great lamentation, for no one believed that Tristram could defeat Sir Marhaus. Tristram rowed himself in a small boat to the island, and once ashore cast the boat adrift. He walked proudly towards Sir Marhaus: 'I shall never run away from you, champion of Ireland. I shall fight until you are slain or I am killed.'

'Proud words, Sir Knight,' replied Sir Marhaus, 'but I shall fight no man who is not of noble blood.'

'Do not fear on that score,' retorted his challenger. 'I am Sir Tristram, the son of a king and the nephew of the same king of whom you demand tribute.'

As the two knights drew nearer, their swords drawn, they hurled abuse at each other until both men raged like angry lions. They wheeled slowly round each other in wide circles, each man protecting his body with his shield. Now and then one would try a sword-thrust to break the other man's defence. But the two warriors seemed to be of equal, and immense, skill. Impatient to strike the first blow, the impetuous Tristram rushed at Sir Marhaus, his sword ringing against the steel that covered his adversary's mighty chest. Soon they were hitting each other blow for blow, and the sea breeze carried a terrible sound from the island to the people waiting on land and on the Irish ship.

For two hours the knights struggled ferociously. 'Brave knight,' gasped Sir Marhaus, who was not a young man, 'let us pause and rest before continuing our fight.'

'With pleasure,' replied Tristram, adding with youthful pride, 'but I can still fight, for I am young and do not lack for breath.'

His momentary lapse of concentration gave Sir Marhaus the opening he needed. He swiftly thrust at Tristram with his sword and pierced him through the opening in his armour between his shoulder and breast plate.

As Tristram staggered from the blow Sir Marhaus jeered, 'I am victor. Nothing can save you now, Sir Tristram, for my sword was smeared with a poison to which there is no antidote. My sister, the Queen of Ireland, brewed this poison, and she does not leave anything to chance when she fears that her brother may be slain.'

Never had anger seized any man as violently as anger now seized Tristram. With a terrible groan he gripped his sword in both hands and let fall on Sir Marhaus' head a savage blow. Sir Marhaus immediately fell to the ground dead. The force of the blow had cut right through his helmet and Tristram's sword was now firmly embedded in the dead knight's head. He struggled to withdraw the blade, and as he did so the tip of the blade broke, remaining in Sir Marhaus' skull.

'I am victor,' roared Tristram. His cry echoed across the sea where it was heard by the waiting crowd of supporters, who struck out rapidly for the island.

The men of Ireland arrived at the island first and they lamented at the sight of their dead champion. Swiftly they took his corpse on board their ship and sailed away from Cornwall. When Sir Marhaus' body was carried into the Irish court, his sister Queen Isoud could not contain her grief. As she washed and dressed his body for the grave she swore vengeance on the slayer of her brother. And when she found the point of the sword in her brother's wound she wrapped it in a cloth and laid it in a chest which she locked.

The Cornish court rejoiced at Tristram's victory. However, Tristram grew weaker daily, for the poisoned wound would not heal. He realized that the only person who could possibly cure him was the Irish queen, Isoud. But yet he knew that if he presented himself as Tristram, the slayer of her brother, he could expect no aid from her – rather death. So Tristram decided to go to the Irish court in disguise. Dressed as a wandering minstrel and calling himself Tramtris, he embarked for Ireland. On landing, Tristram made his way slowly to the Irish court. He was made welcome and soon his playing of the harp had captivated the whole court.

Queen Isoud, moved by the plight of this sick minstrel, asked him how he came by his wound.

'I suffered it in a fight to save the honour of a fair lady,' lied Tristram.

'And were you victorious?' asked the queen.

'Yes. But this did not win me my lady's favour. So I wander and play my harp and sing of my sad love.'

The queen asked to see Tristram's wound. She examined it and told him she could heal it. This she did and as she tended Tristram she grew to like him more and more and was pleased to see his condition improving.

Tristram asked her what favour he could do for her in return. The queen could not immediately think of any favour, but then she had an idea: 'You know we marvel at your skill on the harp. I wish you would teach Iseult, my daughter, to play like you.'

Now Tristram had never seen the queen's daughter, for as befitted a royal princess she had been brought up in almost total seclusion. But he had heard much talk of her beauty. Men would sigh when they mentioned her name, calling her '*La Beale Iseult*' – the beautiful Iseult. Tristram was curious to see her and so he readily agreed to do this favour for the queen.

When he first saw Iseult, he could not believe his eyes. Not only was she tall and noble in her bearing, like all the royal women in this land, but her hair, as black as the raven, was of amazing beauty; her skin was as white as snow and her lips as red as blood. Yet Iseult was not proud: the expression in her eyes was soft and gentle. And Tristram, who had never before been moved to love a woman, fell deeply in love.

The hours between one lesson and the next could not pass quickly enough for Tristram: soon he lived only for the time he would be with Iseult again. He had to remind himself continually that even though he was a prince, he was at the Irish court in disguise as Tramtris: if he were to let slip his identity he might never see Iseult again. And so he kept his love hidden.

Meanwhile Iseult, too, had fallen in love, and could think of no one but her teacher. Yet she did not dare speak of her love for she thought Tramtris still loved the lady for whom he had fought, and secretly wondered whether she was the woman for whom he played his love-songs.

Soon the couple could not bear a day to pass when they did not meet. If the weather was fine they would roam through the countryside nearby. Sometimes Tristram would imitate on his harp the sound of the surf breaking upon the shore on which they walked, or play a flurry of notes that sounded like the wind rustling through the leaves.

When it was wet the teacher and his pupil would sit by the fire, and the walls of the chamber would reverberate with the stirring rhythm of warriors' marching songs. But it was neither the thought of battle nor the heat of the fire that caused their young faces to flush.

No one can say how long this state of affairs might have continued had not fate intervened. One day, as Iseult and Tristram were playing their harps together, the queen found Tristram's sword, which he had left carelessly out of its scabbard. As she picked it up, an icy dread spread through her heart, for she saw the sword had no point. No two swords could be the same, she thought, and she quickly carried it to the room where she had kept the piece of metal she had taken from her brother's wound. The two pieces fitted together. She rushed to the king and told him that she suspected the minstrel Tramtris to be the knight Tristram, slayer of her brother. King Anguish was dismayed at the news, for he too had grown to look with favour on Tramtris. He summoned the unsuspecting minstrel and asked him if he was Sir Tristram. And Tristram told them his whole story.

King Anguish and his queen were now in a quandary: what could they do now about their vows of vengeance? The Tristram they hated and the Tramtris they loved were the same person. After careful thought, King Anguish found the solution. He judged that when Tristram had slain Sir Marhaus he had simply been acting as any knight and champion should have done for his king. They could not punish Tristram for this deed, but they decided that he must leave their castle and return to Cornwall. This Tristram said he would do, but he left with a heavy heart. Before he departed, however, he promised King Anguish that if ever he should need a champion, then he would come from wherever he was to do him this service.

When Tristram arrived in Cornwall, he was welcomed with open arms. In the days, months and years that followed, he performed great feats of valour to distract himself from thoughts of Iseult and eventually became the most powerful knight in all the world. But King Mark, who had rejoiced at his nephew's return, now grew to hate Tristram because the evil talk of his courtiers, who were jealous of Tristram, had corrupted his mind. The nobles played on King Mark's increasing hatred, and soon the king could not bear to hear Tristram's name mentioned, nor could he tolerate the sight of him.

The king wracked his brains to find a way of getting Tristram to leave Cornwall. One day he called Tristram to him and told him that he had decided to marry. Since Tristram had talked of nothing but the virtues of the fair Iseult, he wanted his nephew to go to Ireland as his ambassador and ask King Anguish for his daughter's hand in marriage. Tristram was horror-stricken; he cursed himself for having spoken so freely of his beloved Iseult. However, he had not been oblivious of his uncle's changed attitude towards him, and even if this hateful mission had not arisen, he would have wished to leave Cornwall. Obeying his uncle's command, he set out for Ireland.

The Irish king and queen were overjoyed at Tristram's return. And so was their daughter. The tormented Tristram, however, could not bring himself to reveal the reason for his return. While he delayed, a messenger arrived from the court of King Arthur in Britain. He had come to summon King Anguish to appear at Camelot, or send his champion to meet the challenge of a knight, one Sir Blamor, who had accused King Anguish of killing his cousin in cold blood. Remembering his promise to aid the king if the need arose Sir Tristram immediately offered to go and fight on the king's behalf. King Anguish readily took up Tristram's offer of help and promised the young knight that if he emerged victor and avenger of King Anguish's honour he would grant him whatever he wished. And so Tristram left for Camelot, glad of some respite before the task of escorting Iseult back to Cornwall as his uncle's bride.

For several weeks the Irish court waited impatiently to hear the outcome of the contest between Sir Blamor and Tristram. Then Tristram's ship was seen forging through the waves towards Ireland, and the people knew he was victor.

Tristram was given a hero's welcome, and in the midst of the celebrations King Anguish reminded Tristram that he could ask for whatever favour he desired.

Tristram had dreaded this question, but on the voyage back to Ireland he had decided that he could not, in all honour, ask for what he desired most – the hand of Iseult. Instead, he would do as his uncle had commanded him. Now, though the words almost choked him, he faced the king and asked for Iseult's hand in marriage. At these words Iseult's heart soared. But when she heard the doleful words 'for my uncle' she swooned.

The king was bound to keep his promise even though both he and Queen Isoud had hoped that Tristram would ask to marry Iseult. All they could do was to take some comfort from the fact that it was a good match and would cement peace between Cornwall and Ireland.

The moment of departure soon came. But the queen, who knew Iseult was going to a loveless marriage, could not bear to see the expression of sorrow on her daughter's face. So, drawing on all her skills as a herbalist, she mixed a powerful love potion which she placed in a little crystal flask stoppered with a gold seal. She gave this to Iseult's maid Brangwen, explaining what it was and how she might give this to Iseult to drink on her wedding night, just before she was due to retire with her new husband. Then she would look with love on the Cornish king for the rest of her life, and all thoughts of Tristram would disappear from her mind.

Tristram's behaviour as he boarded the ship for the voyage was stern and cold, for only by acting in this way could he find the strength to see through the mission he had begun. On the journey he told Iseult about his uncle and about Cornwall, and how much she would like the land and the people. One stormy night, Iseult asked

him to sing for her once more a lament he had written for his lost love. So, with his heart breaking, his voice soared above the tempest. As he sang, the dark and turbulent sea seemed to echo Tristram's and Iseult's unspoken emotions.

When the motion of the ship became too great Iseult's maid Brangwen left them to lie down, for she was not a good sailor. Braving the elements, Tristram and Iseult remained alone on the deck, knowing that this was the last time they could be alone together. For some time they watched the heavy skies and the violent swell of the sea. But when Iseult grew chilled, her cloak soaked with sea-spray, the couple went below deck. They entered the cabin, and there amidst all the baggage Iseult saw the flask containing the love potion. She picked it up and wondered if it might be some special warming drink that Brangwen was saving for herself. Anxious to bring a smile to the grave face of Tristram, Iseult took up the fateful flask, removed the stopper and poured the contents into a goblet. Mischievously, she suggested they should drink it there and then and wait to see Brangwen's face when she discovered her drink was gone.

Iseult took the first sip and handed the goblet to Tristram for him to drink. No sooner had the potion passed their lips than they realized, with an intensity that bordered on pain, their overwhelming love for each other. Through their veins rushed a wave of ecstasy and they fell into each other's arms.

All too soon the Cornish coast was sighted, and they knew that they must part forever. But Brangwen, now recovered from her seasickness, found the empty flask and understood what had happened. In vain she tried to comfort the unhappy Iseult; indeed it was only through her care that Iseult was prevented from killing herself.

Iseult and Mark were married. But the love of Tristram and Iseult did not diminish with the passing of time, for the queen's potion had been a powerful one. And so, like actors in a tragedy who know that each step they take will bring their destruction nearer, Tristram and Iseult resorted to secret and dangerous meetings. King Mark still hated Tristram, and there is no doubt that if he had discovered their guilty love he would have slain them both. At times, the desperate couple wondered if this would not have been the best end to their infernal situation.

The minstrel looked at his spellbound listeners, hardly able to continue.

'I ask you, fair ladies and gentlemen,' he said, 'not to judge too harshly the doomed love of Tristram and Iseult, for there were forces at work that they were powerless to resist.'

The queen's cheeks were wet with tears. She moved towards the minstrel and asked him gently, 'Are you Tristram?'

'Yes,' he replied. 'I have been exiled from my love and from Cornwall for ten years – ten years which seem like all eternity – and must wander the land telling my tale to those who will listen. For there is no other occupation for which I am fit.'

But Guinevere was a lady of great compassion. She could not bear to see so outstanding a knight brought to such a pass. All at Camelot knew of Tristram's courageous exploits and they vividly remembered the occasion when, with consummate chivalry, he had spared the life of King Anguish's challenger Sir Blamor when he could have killed him.

There was no doubt in anyone's mind that Tristram must be saved from his joyless life as a wandering minstrel.

Tristram was made a knight of the Round Table. Once again he became a questing knight and accomplished many great deeds.

But the love of Tristram and Iseult never ceased and when, after many long years, King Arthur made Tristram and King Mark make peace with each other, Tristram returned to Cornwall to be near his love. The friendship between the uncle and his nephew was fragile, however, and soon the king's former hatred returned. When he saw Tristram and Iseult's happiness in each other's company it was more than he could bear.

One day as Tristram sat at Iseult's knees King Mark crept up from behind and stabbed Tristram. The wound was mortal. As Tristram lay dying at her feet Iseult felt her heart break and when the last breath left Tristram's body she, too, fell down dead.

King Mark was grief-stricken at what he had done and he had the tragic lovers buried in the same grave. In death, at last, their love had triumphed.

COURTLY LOVE

In feudal times the knight's wife was no more than a chattel, and her husband was at liberty to beat her, as contemporary illuminated manuscripts all too often show. In this age of arranged marriages divorce was not permitted by the Church. But if consanguinity, or distant kinship, could be proved, a couple could have their marriage annulled, allowing both parties to remarry. A surprising number of people would suddenly discover that they were distantly related. Even a couple sharing the same godfather or a husband who had married his godfather's daughter would have been able to obtain an annullment. However, during the age of chivalry the knight's attitude towards women underwent a radical change. What distinguished the later knight from his barbarous, feudal predecessor was his growing awareness of courtesy, which is nowhere better seen than in the romantic, but often ludicrous, practices of courtly love.

For the lady to whom the knight had given his heart he would be courageous in battle, gay, witty, clean and well-dressed. For his lady the knight would swear not to cut his hair, drink wine or sleep in a bed; he might even wear a patch over his eye until he had accomplished some deed in her honour. Some knights swore lifelong devotion to ladies they had never even seen. Courtly love was, however, possible only between people who were not married, and was restricted to the knightly class. Yet the old custom of the *droit de seigneur* – the knight's, or lord's, right to be the first to enjoy the favours of his young female serfs – lingered on. This practice and the code of courtly love existed side by side during the Middle Ages.

The courtly love tradition took root in the twelfth century in the warm and peaceful south of France, where troubadours began composing love songs and romances to entertain the pleasure-loving court. The next step was the establishment of courts of love, at which ladies sat in judgement on affairs of the heart. One case brought before such a court concerned a knight who complained that every time he kissed his lady she stuck a pin into his hand. As far as he was concerned he had never behaved less than chivalrously. The court judged in his favour and pronounced the woman's behaviour inexcusable. As a punishment she had to kiss her lover's hand until the wounds she had inflicted were healed.

It was also a lady's mission to spur her knight on to brave deeds. However, one lady, anxious to be rid of a lover's unwelcome attentions, threw her glove into a den of lions saying that if he loved her he would not hesitate to retrieve it for her. The knight did this but, feeling the whole episode had dishonoured him, afterwards demanded to be released from his ties of duty.

When the cause of courtly love reigned supreme a bizarre, albeit shortlived, sect emerged called the Penitents of Love of Poictou. These knights and ladies believed that love could transform one's life. To demonstrate this they dressed in the warmest clothes and furs in the height of summer and gambolled about in the thinnest summer clothes in the depths of winter, claiming that the elements did not touch those who were in the power of love.

SIR LANCELOT

Sir Lancelot was the bravest and most famous knight in all the world. Far and wide, tales of his exploits had lightened many a long, dark winter's evening. Boys would sit and listen wide-eyed, dreaming of the day when they might accomplish deeds as fine as Sir Lancelot's, slaying dragons and giants in battles that lasted several days and finding ways of combating the evil powers of wicked enchantresses. They also loved to hear of his anger, which was never roused unless the cause was just. But one tale which they did not hear, for those who knew it would repeat it only in whispers, was of Sir Lancelot's love for the fair Queen Guinevere.

Ever since he had first arrived at Camelot, Sir Lancelot had loved the queen. Often he had carried her colours at tournaments and undertaken quests to do her honour. To Sir Lancelot, the queen was the finest woman in the world and he could love no other. King Arthur rejoiced in the devotion Sir Lancelot showed to the queen, for he felt it only right that his best knight should serve his queen. The queen, too, loved Sir Lancelot, yet they both knew that if their love should become common knowledge it would only bring shame, dishonour and sorrow to all.

That winter had been harsh at Camelot and the bad weather had kept Sir Lancelot confined within the castle walls. The snow had fallen so thickly that the knights were not able to venture out, even to hunt. For many months the whole country had been shrouded in a silent white blanket of snow.

Within the castle Sir Lancelot had been seeing the queen in secret and with each day his love for her had grown. Sometimes their eyes met across the hall as the queen sat sewing with her ladies. At other times they would brush by each other when crossing on the stairway. When, at last, spring came, and with it the thaw, Sir Lancelot was determined to leave Camelot. He longed to find some new adventure which would both test his knighthood and take him far from the queen.

The very next day as the knights of the Round Table were seated in the great hall a weary traveller arrived at the castle. Without resting he asked to be taken to King Arthur. Before all the assembled knights he explained the reason for his journey: a young maiden was being held prisoner in a bath of scalding water in the tower of a far-off castle. She had been held there for five years under a powerful spell, because an evil enchantress had thought her too beautiful. He could not say how she had survived so long, but her people now feared for her life.

'Great King, I have made this journey because my fellow countrymen have heard

JulekHeller

that one of your knights surpasses all men in strength, courage and goodness. I beg you, let this knight travel to my country, for he alone can rescue this maiden.'

The traveller's journey had proved too arduous: having made his plea he slumped to the floor, exhausted. The knights ran to his aid, but he was found to be dead.

Everyone present knew which knight he had sought, and all eyes now turned towards Sir Lancelot. Without hesitation he rose to his feet.

'Sire, let this be my quest,' he said. 'I do not know where I shall find this maiden, but I shall ride through the spring rains, the heat of summer and the chill of winter if need be, until I find her. I vow to free her, even if I lose my life in the attempt.'

King Arthur gave his consent, and straight away Sir Lancelot set about making preparations to leave.

Later that evening Lancelot sent his page with a message to the queen's chamber, begging her to see him before he left. He knew that she must come and so he made his way to their secret meeting place.

In the queen's quiet, walled garden, built within the castle and hidden from all prying eyes, Lancelot met Guinevere. She had been weeping. She wrapped her cloak closer around her body. She was not cold but she shivered to think that soon Lancelot, the knight who had loved her and served her so chivalrously, would soon be gone.

The couple moved to sit down on a stone bench. For some time they were silent, listening to the sound of a fountain playing. But when at last they spoke, it was not of their love but of the quest that lay before Lancelot. All too soon it was time for them to return indoors. Lancelot rose and, taking the queen's hand, he kissed it.

'Guinevere, I must leave you because our love can never bring us happiness. If I were to remain here I fear my love for you would drive me mad. But I swear that however long I am gone I shall never cease to love and honour you,' said Lancelot.

'God bless you, Lancelot, and keep you safe,' said the queen. And rising from the bench she crossed the garden to a wooden door set in the wall, unlocked it, passed through the doorway and was gone.

By the next morning all was ready for Lancelot's departure: his armour shone, his refurbished weapons glistened in the morning sunlight and his horse, sensing his master's eagerness to depart, pawed the ground and tossed his head in the air.

As Sir Lancelot rode down from Camelot, King Arthur and Queen Guinevere watched sadly from the castle's battlements, not knowing if they would see this knight again. Sir Lancelot rode onwards, and as he travelled his good spirits were restored, for he was glad to be setting off on a great adventure which would test all his knightly skills. Although he did not know in which land he would find the imprisoned maiden, he felt sure that if he was the knight who could break the spell his wanderings would lead him there. For many days he rode over open plains and through thick forests, asking all whom he met where he could find the country of the unhappy maiden. As he journeyed he stopped only to eat berries growing in the hedgerows and to drink water from streams; at night he slept in the open wrapped only in his cloak, his head resting on his helmet.

For many weeks Sir Lancelot journeyed until one night as he slept, huddled against his horse for warmth, he dreamt he had reached a bleak and desolate country where no living thing flourished and all around was devastation. In this dream he thought he passed through this land until he came in sight of a tower which rose starkly above the rocky landscape, perched on top of a steep cliff. As he looked towards the castle the face of a woman appeared, surrounded by fierce red tongues of fire. She called his name and told him to come quickly. Sir Lancelot awoke with a start, knowing that this was the land and the maiden he sought. Immediately he mounted his horse and rode through what remained of the night, and within the very next day's ride found himself in the ravaged land he had seen in his dream. In the distance he caught sight of the same castle and, spurring on his horse, he galloped towards it. As he rode up a group of bedraggled and emaciated retainers came out to greet him. They hailed him as the man who had come to save their mistress, for only the bravest knight would have undertaken this perilous quest.

'Worthy knight,' they cried, 'how long we have waited for you to come!'

Sir Lancelot dismounted and was led to the tower in which the maiden was imprisoned. But the castle-dwellers would on no account enter. Sir Lancelot bounded up the spiral staircase. As he approached the chamber he felt a great heat

and saw that all the metalwork on the doors was burning hot. Without a thought for himself, he threw his full weight against the doors, at which the locks shattered, the great bolts fell loose and the doors crumbled to the floor. Great clouds of scalding steam and smoke poured over him, and through this choking, burning fog he saw the red flames dancing beneath the tub in which the maiden lay. His eyes began to stream and holding his hand across his mouth he fumbled his way across the room to the bath. He plunged his hands into the boiling water and lifted out the maiden. Looking at her face, he saw she was the woman who had appeared in his dream.

Sir Lancelot's unselfish and courageous deed had broken the spell and the castle folk ventured into the tower. Attendants rushed forward to dress their lady, speedily wrapping her in warm furs. Once clothed, she turned and thanked the knight who had saved her. Sir Lancelot told her his name and she asked him to come with her to her father's castle so she could reward him for her rescue.

The woman told Sir Lancelot that she was Elaine, daughter of the maimed King Pelles, and that this kingdom was known as the Waste Lands. When Sir Lancelot heard this he knew why the land was so desolate. He had heard tales of a country where the king had received a wound which would not heal. Stranger still, men said that when the king was maimed his kingdom, too, seemed wounded for it had withered and remained barren.

Arriving at a graveyard, they reined in their horses so that they could go and thank God for the great deed done that day. As they approached the chapel Sir Lancelot's eye was caught by a tomb on which was inscribed, in letters of gold, the words: 'Here shall come a leopard and he shall slay this dragon and in this foreign country he shall beget a lion.' As he read these words the tomb's lid began to rise and out of it seeped thick black smoke. Within seconds the lid had been cast aside and out of the tomb crawled a dragon with jaws which gaped wide to show its great pointed teeth. Its forked tongue spat out long red and yellow flames and it seemed to crawl and writhe endlessly as its breath lit up its ugly, dark-green, horny scales. Tightening the reins on his terrified horse, Sir Lancelot levelled his lance and looked the creature straight in the eye. As his horse reared its forelegs he delivered a powerful thrust full into the dragon's belly. The monster writhed on its back. But the blow had been true and the dragon, raising its head in one last feeble attempt to break the lance, fell back dead.

The air cleared and Lady Elaine came forward. She led Sir Lancelot into the chapel where they both knelt and gave thanks to God.

'Come, we are near my father's castle,' said Elaine. They rode swiftly and soon they came in sight of it.

But this once-great castle stood half in ruins. Not one of its tall towers stood intact and its massive, crumbling walls gave the only clue to its former magnificence.

Entering the only habitable part of the castle, Sir Lancelot was amazed to meet four young men carrying a bier on which lay a pallid and wizened man. He wore no shirt and the lower half of his body was covered with a red velvet cloth. Sir Lancelot started for he saw then the gaping, livid wound in the king's side.

The king welcomed Lancelot, but before he could thank him King Pelles suddenly fell back on to his couch as if exhausted.

At that very moment a white dove flew in by an upper window. In its beak it held a censor of gold and the air was filled with the sweetest, most refreshing perfume. A light breeze rustled through the chamber and a maiden as beautiful as an angel entered. She carried in her hands a gold chalice which was covered by a gleaming white cloth. Holding the cup high in front of her, she crossed the room and passed through the open doors, which closed behind her of their own accord.

King Pelles appeared to find new strength. 'That was the Maiden of the Grail,' he explained, sensing Sir Lancelot's bewilderment. 'The chalice she carries was used by our Saviour at the Last Supper. The cup was brought into this land by my ancestor Joseph of Aramathia and it has been kept here in Castle Carbonek ever since. Soon a knight is to be born who will be worthy to become its earthly guardian. How I long for that time, for when the good knight comes the wound in my side shall be healed and my wasteland restored to life.'

Sir Lancelot could only marvel at the mysteries of this country. So wrapped in wonder was he that he did not notice how closely King Pelles was observing him.

King Pelles was thinking of a prophecy which a wise man had made many years ago. He had foretold that his daughter Elaine would bear the child of the finest knight in the world, and this child would be destined to become guardian of the Holy Grail. Surely, he thought, the knight now present within his castle was worthy to be father of such a child. Glancing at his daughter, he could see that she loved her rescuer already.

When they all sat down to dine that night Dame Brisene, Elaine's maid, came and stood behind King Pelles' chair. She was regarded throughout the land as the most powerful enchantress, and she told King Pelles quietly how she could make it possible for the prophecy to be fulfilled.

'There are many rumours,' she whispered in King Pelles' ear, 'of Sir Lancelot's love for Queen Guinevere. I can, by my magic crafts, make Lady Elaine appear in the shape of Queen Guinevere and in this guise she can win Sir Lancelot's love.'

King Pelles was troubled by this plan, for it seemed to him base to trick such a chivalrous knight through witchcraft. But he could not forget what wondrous deeds the child of Elaine and Lancelot was destined to achieve. With this in mind he agreed that Dame Brisene should work her magic that very night. And so Lady Elaine retired with Dame Brisene to the enchantress's chamber and the magic spell was cast.

Later that night Sir Lancelot was shown to the guest chamber. A large fire had been lit, filling the room with a warm red glow. Much fatigued, Sir Lancelot lay down beneath the warm covers of the bed and stretched out his tired limbs. Soon he was gently drifting off to sleep. Then he thought he heard the door creaking and, opening his eyes, he saw a shadowy figure enter the room. As the figure walked towards him he saw by the light of the fire that it was a woman. As she moved closer to where Sir Lancelot lay he let out a gasp of amazement: it was Queen Guinevere.

'What magic is this?' he asked in wonder. 'How can you be here? Unless I'm dreaming, answer me, for I must know.' But the figure was silent and would not look at him. He moved to grasp her hand. His fingers touched, and then he dimly saw, the ring that Guinevere wore. He was sure that this was indeed the queen, and that she had at last come to love him.

Next morning Sir Lancelot awoke early. He turned in his bed and, horror-struck, he saw the sleeping figure of Elaine by his side. The colour drained from his cheeks and, letting out a dreadful groan, he leapt from the bed. Like a demented beast trapped in a hunter's pit, he tried to find some way of escape. Elaine stirred and awoke to see him pacing the room in distraction.

'What witchcraft . . . ? What power . . . ? What evil has been at work? What wrong have I done?' he moaned. He could explain nothing to himself.

'Why did you do this to me?' he cried to Elaine. And then she told him of the prophecy.

In a lunatic frenzy Lancelot jumped out of the window and tumbled to the ground, his fall broken only by thorns and brambles which tore into his flesh. Like a wild man he seized an unsaddled horse, mounted it and rode violently away to find some distant place where he could hide his shame.

For many months nothing was heard of Sir Lancelot at Camelot, and when a year had passed all men feared him dead. They grieved much for the loss of the best knight in the world. But his cousin, Sir Bors, was certain that Lancelot was still alive, so he set off in search of Lancelot. At length his journey led him to the wasteland kingdom, where King Pelles told him that Lancelot had at the castle.

'But he is no longer here,' said King Pelles sadly. 'After he came to our land he lost his mind and ran off like a madman into the forest. Since then no man has seen him

but there have been reports of a wild man who roams the forests, and I think that must be Sir Lancelot.'

Now when Sir Bors saw Elaine he noticed that the baby she carried in her arms strongly resembled Sir Lancelot: obviously more had happened in this strange castle than King Pelles was prepared to divulge. Deep in thought, he left to continue his search for Sir Lancelot.

When summer came King Pelles sent his daughter to a distant castle where she might bring up her son, whom she had named Galahad, in peace. Her own home held too many memories for her of Lancelot. She had grown sad after Sir Bors' visit and not even the sight of her little son could cheer her.

Now one day as Elaine and her ladies were playing on the grass beyond the castle walls, one of the ladies threw a ball that they were playing with so hard that it rolled into some trees at the edge of the woods. The lady went to retrieve it, then rushed from the trees in fright.

'Lady, the wild man of the woods is lying dead in the forest,' she explained. 'Let us run away.'

'No,' said Elaine. 'I want to see him.' She walked over to the woods to where the man lay, motionless. The moment she saw him she recognized Sir Lancelot. He was half-starved: his ribs showed through his skin, his cheeks were hollow and his eyes sunken. His flesh was torn and bruised and his hair was long, tangled and grizzled.

Elaine wept to see him but then realized that he was not dead but sleeping. She did not disturb him but immediately rejoined her ladies. 'Quickly,' she ordered, 'fetch men from the castle. This poor man is Sir Lancelot.'

For several weeks Elaine nursed Lancelot and would let no other person near him. In this time he was restored to health. Once recovered, Lancelot felt it his duty to stay with Elaine and made no attempt to leave the castle. Elaine's life was now filled with happiness, and she even tolerated Lancelot's determination never to look at or ask to see his son Galahad.

News of Lancelot's discovery eventually reached Camelot, and Sir Bors once more set out to find him, bringing with him a horse and armour in case Lancelot should wish to return with him. At length he reached the castle and when Lancelot had talked with Sir Bors about Camelot he knew he could no longer stay with Elaine. Sir Bors also spoke of the queen, rekindling Lancelot's love for her. And so Lancelot returned to Camelot, where everyone welcomed him joyously save the queen, who had heard about Elaine's son. But her coldness soon vanished and she found that she now loved Lancelot with an even greater intensity.

When Elaine had watched Lancelot leave her for a second time she was so grief-stricken that she could not even weep, and before long she grew pale and sick. Then, as if in a dream, she took her small son Galahad to a convent and entrusted him to the care of the nuns. She returned to the castle and took to her bed. Soon she was near dying and, summoning her ladies, she ordered them that when she was dead they should clothe her body in her richest garments, place it in a barge and let the barge float down the river to Camelot. Finally she wrote a letter which was to be placed in her hands when she died.

In a little while Elaine died, and her ladies sadly followed her instructions. A black-draped barge containing her corpse was set on the river on the edge of the castle grounds, and the gentle current took it on its journey. Where it passed near the bank autumn leaves fell into the boat, burnishing Elaine's body with their fiery colours.

Finally the barge reached Camelot, where everyone came to look at the beautiful woman lying in the boat now lodged against the river bank. The letter was taken from her hands and given to King Arthur. He opened it and read: 'Sir Lancelot, know that Elaine, whom some men thought fair, never ceased to love you. Mourn for me and see me buried and pray for my soul as you are a true knight.'

Sir Lancelot did as charged and mourned for this gentle woman who had loved him in vain. But her death cast a shadow over his life which time was never to erase.

HERALDRY

When knights were wearing their helmets it was virtually impossible to identify who they were. For this reason they began to paint devices on their shields, and often repeated the same image on their helmets as a crest. It has been suggested that the idea of these devices was taken from infidels seen during the First Crusade, on whose shields were painted wild beasts symbolizing the bearer's warlike characteristics or some other fanciful design.

Early devices were simple and usually in a single colour: the fleur-de-lys of France and the three lions of England are examples. Some early devices punned on the knight's name: if his name was Bull he would paint a bull on his shield; if Heron, Wolf or Salmon those creatures would be depicted. There are less obvious examples, too: the blazon of the English name Wingate was a portcullis, because that word means, from the Latin, 'windy gate'. Some devices recalled a specific incident. A tradition within one family was to present a cup of wine to the English king at his coronation, so their arms depicted the device of three covered silver cups.

The devices, at first purely personal, became hereditary, the son retaining the device of his parent within the device painted on his own shield. This became important when it became necessary to prove noble descent before being declared eligible for knighthood. Knights became obsessed with their genealogy and tried to trace their ancestry back to Adam. They took fierce pride in their crests, which would also be used on their seals, and would kill anyone they thought had taken their crest or was wearing one to which he held no rights.

The main adjudicators of such disputes were the heralds. Originally the officials who proclaimed the results at tournaments, by the mid-thirteenth century heralds had established themselves as the experts on what crest each knight should wear. They became responsible for working out genealogies, devising new arms and passing on their knowledge to apprentices. They developed a special vocabulary of their own, using many French words (argent, dormant, gules, and so on).

Often heralds were the only people who could identify the slain after a battle. After the battle of Crécy in 1346 three heralds and two secretaries were able to draw up a list of eleven French princes and 1,200 knights who had been killed in battle from their heraldic devices alone.

THE GRAIL LEGEND

Although medieval knights could act with savage cruelty and remain unmoved by scenes of carnage, they considered themselves at heart God-fearing men. They would feel no shame at being seen to weep at the sight of some holy shrine to which they had made a long pilgrimage. Religious legends exerted a potent influence on men in the Middle Ages, and cults attached to saints and relics were widespread throughout Europe. No one doubted, for example, that Mary Magdalene had travelled, after the death of Christ, from the Holy Land to Provence in the south of France.

Medieval men also believed in the Holy Grail, which was for them both a physical entity and a mystical source of spiritual nourishment to be attained by only the purest of men. There were two different ideas of what the Grail really was. In one version, the Grail was a stone with magic powers which was housed in the mysterious castle Montsalvat in the Pyrenees. This stone was believed to have fallen from Heaven during Lucifer's struggle with the angels. In another version, the Grail was the cup used at the Last Supper, in which Joseph of Aramathia had caught Christ's blood during the Crucifixion. He is said to have sailed from the Holy Land bringing the Holy Grail with him. Some legends say he travelled only as far as Europe, but others tell how he sailed on to Britain. On landing there Joseph and his band of missionaries made their way to what is now Glastonbury Tor, which rises four hundred feet above the Mendip Hills in Somerset. Here Joseph rested, planting his hawthorn staff in the ground. The staff immediately sprouted white flowers. Joseph determined to stay there and found a church, and hid the Holy Grail in a place nearby.

In 1184 an ancient church built in this place was burnt down and during the re-building the monks discovered what they believed to be the graves of King Arthur and Queen Guinevere. From this moment the legends of Arthur, the quest for the Holy Grail and Glastonbury were inextricably linked. Some believed Glastonbury to be none other than the Isle of Avalon (the legendary burial place of King Arthur), for the land surrounding the Tor had once been marshland, though long since drained. Further mystery arose when in 1345 Joseph's tomb was said to have been found at Glastonbury.

The ruins of the abbey may still be seen today. In its grounds the Glastonbury thorn flourishes still. This strain of hawthorn flowers in winter: is it perhaps descended from Joseph's staff? Finally there is the Chalice Well, in the abbey grounds. This well is said never to have run dry and is thought by some to be the place where Joseph hid the Grail.

SIR GALAHAD

It was the day before Pentecost and all the knights of the Round Table were returning to Camelot to celebrate this great feast day. That evening, as the knights assembled, a damsel rode at great speed into the courtyard.

'Where is Sir Lancelot?' she asked. He was pointed out to her and she rode up to him and said: 'Quickly, take your horse and ride with me into the forest.'

'Why?' asked the puzzled Sir Lancelot.

'I shall explain as we ride. But hurry, there is no time to be lost.'

Sir Lancelot went with the woman and the two riders rode furiously through the forest. It was dark but the woman seemed to know exactly where they were going.

As they rode she explained her mission: 'I come from King Pelles. He bids me tell you that the time is at hand when the Holy Grail shall be seen in this land. Soon the Grail will come to Camelot, but before then there is a sight which you must see.'

Their journey ended when they reached an abbey standing in a forest. They dismounted and the damsel led Sir Lancelot inside. The Abbess came to greet him.

'Welcome, Sir Lancelot. We have in our care a youth of King Pelles' royal blood who has been with us since he was a baby. Naciens, the hermit at King Pelles' castle, has instructed him in the use of arms. We beg you to make him a knight, for there is no knight nobler than you,' said the Abbess.

When the youth was brought in Sir Lancelot beheld the fairest and noblest youth he had ever seen.

'I will knight him gladly,' said Sir Lancelot. He had realized that this youth must be his son Galahad, who had been born to the Lady Elaine in the mysterious Castle Carbonek. That same night Galahad made his vigil and early the next morning Sir Lancelot gave him a father's blessing, and dubbed him knight.

'Will you return to Camelot with me?' asked Sir Lancelot. 'I must return there today for the feast of Pentecost.'

'No,' replied Sir Galahad. 'But I shall come to Camelot soon.'

Sir Lancelot returned to Camelot and joined the knights gathered at the Round Table in the great hall. Each knight was seated and on the back of each seat, written in letters of gold, was the knight's name. One seat remained vacant, however: this was the 'Siege Perilous' or the Seat of Danger. There was no name on the back of this seat, for the wizard Merlin had placed a spell on it and so strong was his magic that to sit in the chair meant certain death to all save the knight for whom it had been made.

On this day the knights saw that letters were forming on the chair: the words told them that the knight to occupy this place was now approaching Camelot. The knights were unsettled by this sight, and so King Arthur ordered a silken cloth to be thrown over the seat.

It was a custom that before the knights began the feast that took place at Pentecost they should first witness an adventure. This time no such event had taken place and they were about to forgo this custom when a squire burst into the great hall.

'Sire, come and see,' he said. 'There is a miraculous sight down on the river. Lodged against the bank is a mighty red stone and in it is fixed a wonderful jewelled sword.'

The knights raced down to the river to see this sight and Arthur read the words that were engraved on the blade: *For the best knight in the world.*

'Surely this sword is for you, Lancelot? Try to draw it out of the stone,' suggested Arthur.

But Lancelot knew that this sword was not meant for him and he would not try to draw it out. Then the king asked Sir Gawain to try but he would not attempt this deed either. They looked a little longer at the sword and then returned to start their feast. All were well pleased that they had seen this strange sight.

They had scarcely started to eat when the old hermit Naciens, accompanied by Sir Galahad, entered the hall. All marvelled at the appearance of this young knight dressed in dark red armour with a magnificent cloak thrown around his shoulders.

Without a word Naciens led Galahad to the Siege Perilous and, pointing to the seat, said: 'I bring you the knight born to sit in the Siege Perilous.'

He pulled the cloth off the Seat of Danger and there the assembled company saw, in still-forming letters of gold, the words '*Sir Galahad, the High Prince*'.

Sir Lancelot looked on proudly as his son took his seat. All wondered at this youthful knight who now sat in their midst. What glorious deeds he would one day achieve, they thought, for he must possess great goodness to be worthy to sit in the Siege Perilous. However, King Arthur's heart grew heavy when he looked at the assembled knights, for he remembered that Merlin had foretold that when all the seats were filled the fellowship of the Round Table would soon be broken.

When the feast was over King Arthur led Galahad down to the river bank to show him the sword in the stone.

Sir Galahad, not surprised, said: 'My sword! The hermit said I should find my sword here.' He flung back his cloak and showed that he was indeed wearing a scabbard without a sword in it. Galahad bent down towards the red stone and with ease drew the sword from it.

When all the knights were seated again at the Round Table they heard a resounding crack of thunder. Suddenly a roaring wind swept through the castle. It swirled round the hall, causing the great wooden doors to slam shut. The candles flickered. All save Sir Galahad sprang to their feet. Some rushed to the doors, others turned to seize their weapons, fearing a surprise attack. Then they stood motionless, for the hall was filled with a beam of light seven times stronger than that of the sun on the brightest summer's day. The knights returned to their seats.

Then a dove flew in through an upper window. As the knights gazed up at it in awe the air was filled with a wonderful perfume. The knights breathed in this air and looked in amazement at their companions. Never had they felt so contented and at peace. Suddenly, there appeared in their midst a golden chalice floating on a beam of light and veiled by a luminous shimmering white cloth. All the knights knew at once what this was: the Holy Grail. Even as they gazed upon it the Grail vanished as mysteriously as it had appeared. There was no sound or movement in the hall.

Sir Gawain was the first to break the silence: 'God be praised for what we have just seen,' he said. 'I cannot rest until I have searched every corner of this land to find the place where I may see the Grail again.'

'I swear this, too,' said Sir Lancelot, 'for the vision we have just seen tells us that the Grail is to be found somewhere within our country. What Christian knight can rest until he has braved danger to find and guard this holy chalice?'

Immediately the whole chamber resounded as the voices of the knights united in a cry of 'The Holy Grail!' King Arthur wept, for it was now as Merlin had foretold: the coming of the Grail into his kingdom would lead to the quest which would take his knights from him. Arthur rose to his feet and looked at his men, whose faces bore witness to the strength of their resolve.

'I cannot deny you this quest, good knights. Let this holy quest last for a year and a day,' said Arthur. He could speak no more, so great was his emotion.

The knights decided to depart the very next day. All night long they made ready.

Morning broke to a clear and rosy sky, and the knights knelt to receive a blessing. They mounted their horses, then rode away without a backward glance. The air rang with the jangling of harnesses and the ground hummed with the sounds of the horses' hooves as they danced along the way. But the knights were silent, thinking only of their purpose – to find the Holy Grail.

Never had the world seen so glorious a sight as this band of knights riding forth over the open land below the castle; in the golden morning light they seemed to shine like the sun when it first beams its light on the sleeping world.

On the second morning of their quest the knights split into groups of twos and threes and rode off in different directions. Sir Galahad, however, rode alone. He travelled for many days without meeting any adventure. Across moors, through plains, up hill and down dale he travelled, until he came to a monastery deep within a forest. He was welcomed by the monks, and on being taken to the guest room he found that two other knights, Sir Ywain and King Bagdemagus, were already there. They greeted each other and Sir Galahad asked what had brought them to this place.

'We made our way to this monastery because on our quest we heard tales of a miraculous shield that is said to hang in the chapel here,' said King Bagdemagus. 'The rumours say that it can be carried only by the best knight in all the world, and this shall be the man who succeeds in the quest for the Holy Grail.'

'But,' said Sir Ywain, 'if the shield is taken down by an unworthy man, within three days he shall meet with some great misfortune, and the shield shall be returned to the chapel to await the time when the best knight comes to claim it.'

'I know I am not the best knight but I am determined to take the shield and see what adventure follows,' said King Bagdemagus. 'Why not remain here for three days, Sir Galahad? If I fail in this adventure and the shield is returned here, I can think of no worthier knight than you to claim it.' Sir Galahad agreed that he would do this.

Next morning the three knights went to the chapel to look at the shield. It was very large, and bore a red cross on a pure white ground. King Bagdemagus took it down from where it hung above the altar. He mounted his horse and rode off into the forest accompanied only by his squire, who followed at a short distance behind him.

King Bagdemagus had not been riding for very long when he saw before him a knight clad in dazzling white armour. The knight's lance was levelled, and he was charging straight at Bagdemagus. King Bagdemagus immediately levelled his lance and spurred his horse forward to engage in combat with this strange knight. They

pounded towards each other, the ground shaking under the thud of their horses' hooves, and although King Bagdemagus was a mighty warrior his lance did not come near his opponent's armour. But the White Knight's lance found its mark square on King Bagdemagus' chest, for the shield did not protect him. The king was thrust from his horse and fell senseless to the ground, while his squire rushed forward to aid him.

'This knight was proud and foolish to think that he could wear this shield,' said the White Knight. 'Take him up gently and bring him back to the monastery. Also take with you this shield and give it to the pure knight, Sir Galahad. Do not ask how I know he is there, but tell him that he alone is worthy to carry this shield.'

The squire led the wounded king back to the monastery. He gave the shield to Sir Galahad telling him what the mysterious White Knight had said.

'Make me a knight. I am nobly born. I am Melias, the son of the King of Denmark,' the squire begged Sir Galahad.

'Fair Melias, I will do that for the service you have done me in bringing me this shield,' said Sir Galahad. 'I hereby make you a knight. Now, Sir Melias, come, ride with me until some adventure separates us.' Sir Melias went willingly with Sir Galahad.

They rode off into the forest and before long the White Knight appeared before them. The two knights marvelled at the sight of him, for the light reflected by his shimmering suit of armour made it seem as if he rode on a sunbeam. Sir Galahad greeted him and, looking at his shield, asked the knight to tell him from where it came.

'This shield was made long ago in the holy city of Sarras by Joseph of Aramathia, who brought it into this country. Before he died he drew the cross upon it with his blood and instructed that it be hung in the monastery from which you have just come, until it should be claimed by a holy knight. Good Sir Galahad, your life has been without greed and pride, and you are worthy of this shield. Continue on your quest, for your goodness shall ensure that you prosper in all that you seek,' said the White Knight. Then he turned his horse and rode into the trees, and in an instant he had completely vanished.

Sir Galahad was amazed at what he had just heard, and seemed for a while lost in thought. But soon the two knights continued on their journey. They rode on through the forest until the path divided into two ways. They halted and an old man came forward.

'Sir knights, you must each choose a way forward,' said the old man. 'The path to the right leads to a safe journey's end. But the path to the left is difficult and dangerous for all but the bravest knight.'

'I shall take the path to the left,' said Sir Melias, for he longed to prove how worthy a knight he was. He rode quickly down this path before Sir Galahad could stop him.

Sir Melias rode for two full days until he reached a meadow. Here, resting beneath a cluster of trees he saw a throne on which rested a gold crown. He went nearer and saw that the ground beneath this throne was covered with cloths on which lay many delicious dishes of food. He dismounted and ate, and as he went to mount and ride away he took the crown from the throne.

As he moved away he saw a knight riding towards him.

'Thief! Set down that crown and make ready to defend yourself,' shouted the knight. Before Sir Melias had time to steady his horse the knight had charged upon him, wounding him in the side with a spear. Sir Melias fell to the ground, near dying. His adversary rode up and, catching the crown up with his sword, made to ride away.

Sir Galahad's path, to the right, had brought him to this same meadow, and he arrived just in time to see the strange knight attack the unprepared Sir Melias. He grew angry when he saw his wounded companion.

'Turn and fight, cowardly knight,' commanded Sir Galahad. 'I shall strike you from your horse for so basely attacking this young knight.'

The knight wheeled his horse round and rode furiously at Sir Galahad. Soon the air was filled with the sound of their clashing swords. Rising in his saddle, Sir Galahad struck his opponent such a blow that the knight tumbled to the ground.

'I yield to you,' groaned the knight. He pulled himself up on one elbow and when he saw it was Sir Galahad who had defeated him he said, 'Good Sir Galahad, I was bound to overthrow this knight for his pride in choosing the left-hand path and for his greed in taking the crown. Although I am dressed in armour I am a hermit and I shall heal Sir Melias' wounds. Continue on your quest, for you trust in God to lead you to your journey's end – not, as this wounded knight has done, on your pride in your own strength.

Sir Galahad left the hermit and continued on his quest. Throughout the kingdom stories of this brave knight's achievements reached the other questing knights, and many of them tried to find Sir Galahad in order to ride with him, knowing that if they did so they would not only gain great glory for themselves but would also, surely, succeed in the quest of the Holy Grail.

One night as Sir Galahad rested in the open, a damsel rode up to him.

'Sir Galahad, come quickly with me. Sir Perceval and Sir Bors are waiting for you nearby on an enchanted ship, which is ready to take you further on your journey to the place where the Holy Grail rests. Hurry, for without you the ship cannot set sail.'

Without a word Sir Galahad leapt up and rode off with the damsel to a small creek in which the enchanted ship lay at anchor.

This mysterious ship was hung with translucent white sails which glistened in the darkness. No sooner had Sir Galahad and the maiden boarded the vessel than it moved from the shore. There was no crew to man it, yet this boat seemed to know its own course. Soon it had left the creek and was sailing on the open sea.

The three knights were delighted to be reunited and each man told of the many adventures which had led them to this wonderful ship. But they had no idea from where this ship had come. Then the maiden explained: 'This ship carried Joseph of Aramathia to Britain when he brought the Holy Grail to this land. It has appeared upon the seas once more in order to carry you worthy knights nearer to the place where you will find the Grail.'

For several days the enchanted ship rode on the open sea until one morning the knights awoke to find the boat moored by a rocky shoreline.

Bidding the maiden farewell, the three knights made for the shore, where they found horses waiting for them. They rode inland and soon reached the devastated land of King Pelles. As they drew near to his castle the inhabitants came out to greet them. The three men dismounted and entered the hall of the castle.

Inside they saw the frail figure of the maimed King Pelles. He was lying on a

couch and the great wound in his side was clearly visible. He feebly raised himself.

'Greetings, Sir knights,' he said, and he wept to see his grandson Sir Galahad arrive in such splendour. 'The end of your quest is near, for tonight the Holy Grail shall be in this castle.'

As night fell an unearthly wind rushed through the castle.

'Let all unworthy men leave this chamber,' ordered King Pelles. All departed save the three knights and the king. As they waited expectantly, the room was filled with an overpowering heat and the doors burst open to admit an unearthly procession of heavily veiled figures. As they glided across the hall, hardly seeming to touch the ground, the knights looked on in wonder. The first two figures carried tall lighted white candles in heavy gold candlesticks. The figure following them held aloft a flat silver dish. Behind them was a figure, its head bent forward, carrying a spear. From the tip of this spear fell drops of blood, but the drops never touched the ground: instead, they mysteriously vanished. The final figure carried the vessel of the Holy Grail, which shone through the same gleaming white veil as that the knights had seen on the first occasion at Camelot.

The figures gracefully crossed the floor and each in turn placed the candlesticks, dish, spear and the vessel of the Grail on a silver table which had been brought in preparation for this event. As the figures turned from the table to move away and merge into the shadows their angelic faces were momentarily visible.

The knights knelt, filled with an overwhelming sense of peace and tranquillity.

Then a mighty voice rang out: 'Draw near the Grail, Sir Galahad, for all your life has been a preparation for this moment. You are without pride, greed, cowardice and all the weaknesses of men. Drink from the cup, Sir Galahad, earthly guardian of this most sacred relic. Guard it well, so that only worthy men may look upon it in its full glory. For in it they will glimpse the paradise which all men seek.'

Sir Galahad approached the table and with great reverence drew off the cloth. He lifted the vessel in both hands, raised it slowly to his lips and drank. As he returned the cup to the table, the assembled company knelt and praised God for the sights they had seen. At length Sir Galahad rose and looked towards his grandfather. Without a word he moved to where the king lay on his couch. Sir Galahad bent down and placed his fingers on the wound in King Pelles' side. Straight away the gaping wound closed and was healed. King Pelles immediately rose to his feet and joyfully embraced Sir Galahad. Exactly as prophesied, the king's grandson had healed his wound and now his wasteland kingdom would be restored to life.

Once again the voice filled the hall: 'Sir Galahad, make ready to leave this land. Tonight the Holy Grail shall pass from the kingdom of Logres, for the men in this land have grown wicked and it shall never be seen here again. Take Sir Perceval and

Sir Bors with you as companions on your journey. The enchanted ship awaits you where you left it. You shall escort the Holy Grail to the distant city of Sarras, which shall be the Grail's resting-place.'

The knights at once set out on their journey. From the torches which lit the castle's courtyard they could see that King Pelles' kingdom had come to life once again, for the air was filled with the sweet smell of roses which had suddenly blossomed.

By daybreak the knights had reached the enchanted ship. No sooner had they boarded than the vessel moved off from the shore, and when they ventured below they found the Holy Grail covered with a gleaming red cloth.

For many weeks the ship sailed its own course at a gentle speed, as if conscious of its precious cargo. At length the knights sighted the city of Sarras and on making land the inhabitants came out to greet them.

In this city the knights built a temple to house the Grail, and when the king of this city died the inhabitants begged Sir Galahad to be their king. Every day the knights went to pray before the Grail. Then one day, as they knelt in prayer, a voice told Sir Galahad to draw nearer to the Grail. As he approached it, a mighty beam of light descended upon him, shining with unbearable intensity, and when it passed the Grail was gone from its resting-place and Sir Galahad lay dead: for the Grail had revealed such wonders to Sir Galahad that he no longer wished to live upon this earth.

Sir Perceval and Sir Bors buried Sir Galahad's body and grieved for this good knight. No longer wishing to stay in Sarras, they both left the city. Sir Perceval became a hermit and spent the rest of his days in seclusion in foreign lands. Sir Bors, however, sailed once again to the kingdom of Logres, where he related to his king the glorious conclusion to the quest of the Holy Grail.

THE CRUSADES

In 1095 reports reached Europe of pilgrims being attacked and harassed by Muslims while on pilgrimages to the shrines of Jerusalem. Further spurred on by pleas for aid from Alexius Comnenus, the Christian Emperor of Byzantium, against invading Turks, Pope Urban II seized this opportunity to attempt to unify the European knights and to cease their warring against each other. In an emotive speech he urged all knights to take up arms against the infidels and regain the Holy City of Jerusalem. Men who died on this quest, he said, would be declared martyrs. Throughout Europe knights immediately 'took up the cross', sewing strips of red cloth in the form of crosses to their cloaks. And so began the greatest adventure that knights were ever to undertake.

Although the motive behind the Crusades was religious many knights no doubt thought of the plunder, land and glory to be won from such an enterprise under the sanction of a holy war. They thought little of the hazards of making a journey into unknown territory to meet an enemy they had never before encountered.

When in 1097 the knights set out they had a lamentable lack of geographical knowledge about the country to which they were going. They slaughtered indiscriminately on their way. As they travelled further East they suffered under the heat, the like of which they had never previously experienced, and many died of sunstroke. Disease was rampant and many knights died before reaching the Holy Land. Their suffering, near-starvation and exhaustion gave rise to visions and outbreaks of mass hysteria.

In 1099 when they first sighted Jerusalem the entire army fell on its knees and they all wept with joy. After a short siege they

stormed Jerusalem on 15 June 1099 and the air was filled with the Crusaders' battle cry, *'Deus le vólt'* (God wills it). Such was the savagery and frenzy of their attack on the people of Jerusalem that as the Crusaders walked victoriously through the streets, weeping with joy to see the most holy shrines of the Christian world, they were said to have waded in blood up to their ankles.

The Crusaders' success served to unite the knights in their feeling of superiority, and for the next two hundred years the Crusades were regarded as the highest cause to which any knight could devote himself.

constantinople
tarsus
antioch
damascus
acre
babiloinne
malloune

THE KNIGHTS TEMPLAR

The Crusades saw the institution of many knightly orders, of whom the Knights Templar were the most celebrated and, in time, the most infamous.

Founded in 1118 to conquer and maintain the Holy Sepulchre in Jerusalem, they built their quarters on the foundations of the ancient temple of Solomon from which they took their name. In 1128 a rule for the order was drawn up by St Bernard of Clairvaux. Templars took vows of poverty (seals of the order show two knights riding on one horse), chastity and obedience. They cut their hair but not their beards. Unlike the Knights Hospitallers, another new order of knighthood set up at this time, they had no obligation to tend the poor or sick. Their sole role was to make war on the infidels.

Soon these warrior-monks, known as the 'militia of Christ', won great fame on the battlefield, where they were marked out by their white mantles bearing a splayed red cross. They were always to the fore in any attack. Their bravery became legendary – they would be neither captured nor ransomed, nor would they ask for mercy, and nor would they retreat unless outnumbered three to one.

Their reputation attracted many young scions of European nobility, and in time they received vast donations in money and land. Although professing personal poverty the Grand Master, head of the Knights Templar, could accept gifts for the order.

As their wealth, power and influence grew, so did other men's suspicions of the Templars. Their wealth undoubtedly led to a relaxation of the order's strict rules and the phrase 'to drink like a Templar' became well-known. They were also suspected of dabbling in the occult.

Templars developed a sophisticated banking system whereby money deposited in one city could be withdrawn in another. They are also credited with being the first to use cheques.

When the Christians were driven from the Holy Land the order moved its headquarters to Cyprus and then to France, but by 1306 Philip IV of France was anxious to be rid of the wealthy and powerful Templars. On Friday 13 October 1307 all the Templars in France – save thirteen – were arrested. They were brought to trial and under torture they confessed that they were guilty of blasphemy, and that their rites of initiation involved spitting and trampling on the Cross, denying Christ and committing other obscene acts. They were also accused of participating in heretical ceremonies which involved the adoration of a mysterious bearded head. This charge could perhaps refer to the relic now known as the Turin Shroud (a shroud dating from the first century AD which bears the image of a crucified man and is thought to be the shroud of Christ), which was believed to be in the possession of the Templars from 1204 to 1307.

Having extracted the confessions, Philip sent over fifty of the Templars to the stake, including the Grand Master, Jacques de Molay. But Philip's persecution could not extend through the rest of Europe and although Templars in England, Spain, Italy and Germany were arrested they did not suffer the same fate as the Templars in France. None the less, in 1312 the order was officially dissolved by Pope Clement V.

Philip of France's intention to obtain for himself the Templars' vast treasure was however thwarted. It disappeared from the order's headquarters in France together with the order's documents on the day of the Templars' arrest. Some believe it was spirited away in galleys belonging to the order.

For centuries men have sought to discover the treasure of the Templars, but it has never been found, nor is anyone sure what it was. Did the Templars find the legendary treasure of the Temple of Solomon in Jerusalem? Was it a fabulous treasure trove of another kind? Was their 'treasure' a mere smokescreen for the possession of some arcane knowledge of occult practices? The answer to the mystery seems to have been lost as surely as the treasure itself.

ST GEORGE

In AD 303, after tearing up edicts of the Emperor Diocletian in the streets, a Christian Turkish soldier known as Nestor of Cappodocia was tortured and martyred. If records are to be believed, he seems to have been martyred on no less than four occasions, being restored to life each time. The courage and faith of Nestor spread and the early Christians gave him the new name of George.

According to legend, on one occasion this brave soldier went to Sileres in the Kingdom of Libya where he found that a dragon was terrorizing the local inhabitants. The dragon, it seemed, could be appeased only by human sacrifices. When George arrived the next victim was to be a beautiful young princess. George sprang to the rescue, killing the dragon on the spot. Other versions of the legend tell how the dragon was pacified and led into the now-freed city by the princess.

The tales of George's exploits appealed to knights, whose ever-fertile imaginations kept alive their belief in dragons and other monsters. As a rescuer of maidens in distress, a scourge of infidels and a warrior prepared to die for Christ, he also seemed to personify the ideals of a Christian knight. In 1222, the English proclaimed 23 April to be St George's Day, and a hundred years later he was adopted as the country's patron saint. 'St George' became part of the English battle cry.

However, the ideals embodied in the legendary figure of St George are not restricted to England. He is also the patron saint of the Greek army and of Greek shepherds and patron saint of the Spanish province of Aragon.

LOHENGRIN

Many hundreds of years ago a band of valiant and good knights devoted their lives to the search for the Holy Grail. The Holy Grail was the sacred cup from which Jesus Christ drank at the Last Supper and it was the most precious and sought-after relic in the world. The Grail possessed great and wondrous powers: it could cure all wounds and heal all sickness, and whoever came to look upon it enjoyed perfect peace ever after. But the cup could only be found by men who had led unselfish lives and had never allowed themselves to yield to wicked thoughts.

Through blazing deserts, rocky lands and icy wastes this band of knights travelled until, at length, they found themselves in the fertile, wooded region surrounding the Mount of Salvat. Here they were filled with an unimaginable content which was so strong that they lost any desire to continue their journey. Then a voice from the heavens told the knights that this was the place where the Sacred Cup rested. There on the mountain the knights built a great castle for the Grail; within those walls the sacred vessel remained, and the knights were ever after known as the Knights of the Holy Grail.

The castle they built reached right up to heaven; its walls were thick and built of stone, and the only entrance was over a drawbridge through great steel doors. The castle was therefore secure against all forms of attack, and only men who were deemed worthy by the knights, the self-appointed guardians of the Grail, were admitted to it. Meanwhile, the knights had abandoned their swords, for within this castle there could be no cause for violence. No foul air, smoke or grime polluted the castle either, for the Grail cleansed the very air around it. It could even provide nourishment: the knights had only to look upon the Grail for whatever they desired to eat and drink to be instantly provided, on golden dishes.

On the topmost tower of this castle was a belfry which housed a large golden bell. At times this bell would ring, and the sound would reverberate throughout the castle. Then the good knights would know that somebody in the world beyond their paradise was in distress and needed their aid. Though none of them knew how this bell was rung, the knights always heeded its summons, and one of them would be chosen to ride out and bring peace to the person in trouble.

The king of this great castle was Parzifal – the simple youth who had grown so wise and good that the knights had joyfully proclaimed him their king. He ruled with great wisdom, always mindful of the sacred trust that had been granted to him.

LOHENGRIN

At this time the land which we now call Germany was made up of many small kingdoms whose monarchs were vassals to the great King Henry. He was a wise king who worked all his life to keep the kingdoms from warring with each other. Reports reached King Henry that there was strife and bitterness in Brabant, which had so recently been ruled in peace by its duke. The old duke had died, leaving as his sole heir his young daughter, the lovely maiden Else. When near death, the duke had entrusted Else to the care of his bravest knight, Frederick of Telramund. He felt sure Frederick would look after the girl's best interests. But it was a rich kingdom and Frederick had soon grown greedy and grasping, wanting the land for himself. He decided to marry Else and rule as duke. The people were greatly disturbed, for they loved Else and wanted her to marry someone she loved – someone who would also care for the country. They disliked Frederick because he thought only of war and they suspected that if he became ruler the land would be drained of its resources and its strongest men taken away by Frederick to wage unnecessary wars.

All this had been relayed to King Henry, who immediately made his way to Brabant to judge whether or not Else should marry Frederick. His job was made more difficult because Frederick had gathered around him a strong and fearsome group of warriors whose brute force might be used to override the course of justice. In an open meadow, seated beneath a spreading oak tree, King Henry sat to hear Frederick and Else plead their cases.

The awesome figure of Frederick came forward. Brimming with confidence he argued that Else was but a weak woman and that her father had made him her guardian. Although nothing had been written down there had been an unspoken understanding, he claimed, that, as day follows night, when the time was right he should wed Else and rule in her stead. Surely, he reasoned, her children would be of the royal blood and worthy to succeed as rulers of Brabant? He vowed that he, Frederick, would make this land famous throughout the world. In conclusion, he asked if the future security of the kingdom was not more important than the feeble objections of a woman.

The king could not dispute the arguments Frederick put forward. Yet he was uneasy, for although Frederick was a brave knight, a valued ally for any man, there was something dark and dangerous about him.

Then Frederick made a suggestion: 'If Else is so against our marriage, let her find a champion to fight me. If defeated, I shall yield to the better man.'

As he finished speaking a hush descended upon the waiting crowd, for now Else came forward like a lovely lily, her head bowed down with sorrow. The crowd exchanged glances of sympathy amongst themselves for they knew that the poor girl feared not only for herself but for the future of her country.

'Great King,' said Else, 'there is very little I can say in my defence. My fears, many will say, are without foundation, for Frederick has done nothing to negate his right to marry me. Yet I have prayed that I shall be spared this fate. And each time I pray, I see my champion, the most valiant knight in the world, who has said he will come to save me.'

'Pah . . . the knight of your dreams,' said Frederick callously. 'If he exists, where is he now? The sooner you marry me and forget these dreams the better for all.'

'My champion *will* come. Of that I am certain,' said Else, with more spirit than any man thought the girl possessed. Turning to the king, she begged him to give her just a few hours more.

King Henry, moved by the girl's passionate pleas, agreed, but said that if Else's knight had not arrived by sunset then she would have to marry Frederick.

As the hours passed, Frederick paced the ground impatiently and Else searched the horizon anxiously, willing her knight to come.

Then the king rose, for the sun, already low on the horizon, had suddenly grown redder and the great trees had cast long evening shadows. He was about to deliver his judgement when Else jumped up and rushed towards the river that flowed at the edge of the meadow.

She cried out and pointed: 'He is coming, he is coming! Look, there on the river is the knight I have seen in my dreams. And he will fight for me.'

Every eye turned and looked where Else was pointing. There upon the river was a beautiful swan; trailing from its beak was a golden cord attached to a little boat, and in the boat stood a tall knight in dazzling silver armour.

'Else's champion has come to save her,' shouted the people. Else scarcely dared to look, so overcome was she.

The knight alighted and bade farewell to the swan, which floated majestically away down the river.

'Greetings,' said the knight, stepping forward. 'I have come in answer to a summons to fight for Else's cause.'

The king welcomed the stranger, then, anxious that the whole business should be settled before the daylight was gone, he ordered the combat to begin.

Frederick strutted forward like a peacock, quite confident that he would have no difficulty in overcoming this knight – though he wondered whether there might be some magic at work: would the knight of Else's dreams vanish into air at his first blow?

To his great surprise he soon found that the newcomer was no figment of anyone's imagination and he had to draw on all his skill to save himself from his assailant's blows. The Knight of the Swan seemed superhuman, and his sword flew through the air with such devilish strokes that they defied all Frederick's cunning defences. What is more, the stranger did not seem to have to move, while Frederick had to dart about to dodge the blows and to fight with all his might.

Frederick, outclassed, was soon exhausted. At last he slipped when avoiding a blow and slithered to the ground with a painful thud. There he lay, furious to find himself in such a ludicrous position. Raising his visor to reveal his grimy face, bathed in sweat, Frederick addressed his challenger: 'Slay me, you miserable knight, for it could only be witchcraft that has made me slip, to lie here at your mercy.'

'Not so,' replied the Swan Knight. 'I did not come here to slay you but to save Else. And this I have now done.'

The king agreed, and while Frederick's squires helped him from the meadow the king took Else and the Knight of the Swan by the hand: 'Else, will you be content to marry the man who has saved you, and share with him the rule of your kingdom?'

'Yes,' answered Else without hesitation.

'You, Sir knight, will you honour this princess and live with her as a husband and guard her well?'

'I will,' the Swan Knight replied, 'on one condition. I ask before you all that Else shall ask me neither my name nor from what country I come, either now or at any time in the future.'

'I promise,' said Else, and the knight inclined his head to kiss her on the brow.

Else and her knight were married the very next day, and from that time the kingdom of Brabant flourished under the couple's just and happy rule. The country grew prosperous and was filled with a happiness that could only have come from some great goodness.

As the years passed Else and her knight had many children, and so accustomed had Else grown to not knowing anything about her knight's past life, or even his name, that she was happy simply to call him 'Husband'.

Frederick, however, had not forgotten his ignominious fall at the hands of this knight. Having left Brabant on the day of his defeat to fight in foreign wars, he now returned after an absence of many years.

Else and her family welcomed him gladly, not suspecting that he could still harbour any grudge against her. But Frederick thought only of how he could break Else's happiness. The only way that occurred to him was to drive Else mad by thoughts of what she did not know about her husband.

Frederick immediately began to cultivate the affections of the couple's children, for they were bright and loving and they delighted to hear of Frederick's adventures in foreign lands. He would tell them of the sights he had seen, of the people who had just one eye and walked on one foot, and of the dragons and monsters who rose out of the sea. The children squealed with delight to hear how he had vanquished these creatures.

But as he told them these tales he would ask them: 'Do you not think it strange that you do not know your father's name? Surely you are curious to know where he comes from, for he is so brave that all his countrymen must be so?'

For many months Frederick insinuated these questions into the children's minds and, as he had hoped, each time he spoke like this they would go to their mother and ask her why she could not tell them all they wanted to know.

LOHENGRIN

Else grew distressed that she could not give her children the answers they wanted. She began to spend wakeful nights sitting and watching her sleeping husband. Through the dark night hours she reflected that although she loved him with all her heart she did not know anything about him.

Frederick noted her pale face and continued to torment her secretly. He would follow her as she walked round the castle and when she stopped pensively by some pillar he would creep up behind her and whisper, 'Who is my husband and what is his land?', and before the startled Else could see who had spoken he had slipped away.

Soon Else could bear it no longer and, whatever the cost, she was determined to ask her husband his name and his country. That evening as the couple were preparing for bed she turned to the Swan Knight and said, 'I cannot endure it any longer, my dearest husband. I *must* know your name and your country, even if only for the sake of our children.'

Else looked at her husband's face and immediately saw that she should not have asked. She dissolved in sobs. He raised her up and, wiping the tears from her face, looked at her sadly.

'You should not have asked me, Else, for now I am bound to leave you. Why could you not have trusted me? Tomorrow in the meadow where I first came to you I shall leave you. But before I do I shall answer your question.'

The next day they went to the meadow. Else was a pitiful sight, her robes dishevelled and her braids undone, her face like a death's head with staring, fevered eyes. Her children clung to her skirts, frightened by their mother's strange appearance. Then her husband came to her. He kissed his children and his wife, and handed her his sword, his ring and his hunting horn.

Then, standing a little way off, he announced his identity: 'I am Lohengrin, the son of Parzifal, the King of the Castle of the Holy Grail on Mount Salvat. Many years ago the bell rang in the castle's tower and summoned me to come and give you aid. I am a Knight of the Grail and it is from this alone that I derive my strength and wisdom. This was how I was able to build your land into the great kingdom it is. But, my beloved wife, I have this strength only when this knowledge is my secret alone. Your question has forced me to disclose the truth and I am now bound to return to Mount Salvat and leave you forever.'

Lohengrin ceased speaking and the swan once again appeared on the water drawing the boat. Lohengrin stepped aboard. As the boat moved out into the stream, he stood motionless, without casting so much as one glance towards the grieving Else. Soon the boat and the swan were out of sight, leaving behind only an afterglow of unearthly radiance.

THE DEATH OF ARTHUR

Civil war had cast its dark shadow over King Arthur's kingdom. Mordred, the king's bastard son, had long sought to bring about the destruction of the Round Table and now, at last, one of the plans of his diseased mind had born tragic fruit. Together with a band of knights, Mordred had trapped Lancelot in the queen's chamber and, after a murderous struggle, Lancelot had escaped leaving the queen to Mordred's mercy. Guinevere was brought before King Arthur to stand trial for her adultery. King Arthur, who had striven so hard to establish law and order in his kingdom, was now forced to pass the sentence of death on his queen.

The morning after her trial Guinevere, clad in only her shift, was led to the stake by Sir Gareth and Sir Gaheris. They grieved at the heavy duty they had been ordered to perform, and would not carry their swords but instead dressed in robes of deepest mourning.

As the first torch was put to the bundles of firewood Sir Lancelot rode forward with a band of followers. He fought his way to the queen, cutting down many knights as he went, freed Guinevere and carried her off to safety. But Lancelot did not know that in saving the queen he had slain the unarmed Gareth and Gaheris, brothers of Sir Gawain.

Arthur was at first consumed with anger, but his anger soon abated. The love he still bore for Guinevere and Lancelot made him glad that they had escaped death. Soon Lancelot returned Guinevere to the king, and a troubled peace ensued.

But Sir Gawain brooded on his brothers' deaths. His former love and esteem for his brother knight Sir Lancelot had turned to hate and he sought for revenge. Enlisting the unwilling support of King Arthur, he mustered an army and crossed into France to wage war on Sir Lancelot, who had travelled to his castle there. King Arthur, oblivious of his son's evil intentions, left Mordred to rule Britain while he was gone.

Close by Sir Lancelot's castle a fierce battle took place in which Sir Gawain was killed. Then grave news came from England: Mordred had usurped the throne and intended to take Guinevere for his wife. Straight away Arthur returned to reclaim his kingdom. Surrounded by only a small band of knights he made camp and waited to do battle with his son.

As Arthur slept the night before the battle Sir Gawain appeared to him in a dream and warned him that if he took part in the fighting the next day he would be slain. Next morning, careless of his own safety but anxious that no knight should fall beneath the sword of his brother knight, the great king sued for peace with Mordred. Finally, even though the two battle lines were drawn up, a fragile truce was made. But neither Arthur nor Mordred trusted the other's words, and each man instructed his forces that if a single sword be drawn battle should commence immediately.

As Mordred and Arthur were ratifying the treaty with cups of wine, an adder slid from the undergrowth and bit one of Mordred's knights on the foot. Without a thought this knight drew his sword, and as he raised it in the air to strike a blow to kill the snake, the sun caught his blade and made it glint – a sight witnessed by both the waiting armies.

Immediately the war trumpets sounded and the two sides charged into battle. They fought through a whole day. Many brave men fell lifeless to the ground as knights who had once been joined in the same brotherhood now fought each other to the death.

The exhausted Arthur rallied to see who among his knights remained alive. There were but two, Sir Lucan and Sir Bedivere, and Arthur's heart grieved. The wicked Mordred sought out his father, for he wished to see him dead. At last he saw him and rushed forward. Arthur stood motionless and as Mordred hurled himself on Arthur, he dashed himself upon his father's sword. But as he fell, mortally wounded, he brought down his sword on Arthur's head.

Arthur knew he had not long to live, and remembering Merlin's words he asked the good Sir Bedivere to carry him to a place away from the battlefield. As he lay above the plain on which the battle had been fought he gave his sword, Excalibur, to Sir Bedivere and told him to take it and cast it into the waters beyond. For he knew he soon would pass into the vale of Avalon – the place where his wounds would be healed.

Sir Bedivere rode away, but when he reached the water's edge he could not bring himself to cast Excalibur into the water. And so, hiding it beneath a tree, he returned to Arthur and told him he had done as instructed.

'And what did you see?' asked Arthur.

'Nothing but the still waters covering the sword as it fell,' answered Sir Bedivere.

'You lie,' gasped Arthur. 'Return and do this last service for me.'

Filled with shame, Sir Bedivere returned to where he had left Excalibur. He took up the sword and once again rode towards the water. Holding the great sword by its pointed blade he hurled it with all his might out over the waters. As the sword somersaulted through the air a pale and glistening arm emerged from the water. The sword fell straight into this waiting hand, and no sooner did the hand grasp it than it was drawn beneath the water.

Sir Bedivere returned to where he had left the king, but Arthur was no longer there. Looking out across the dark waters where the sun was sinking in the west, its last rays turning the water a fiery red, Sir Bedivere saw silhouetted against the sun a barge with a single sail. As it moved slowly through the waves, he saw that it carried four black-veiled women supporting the body of King Arthur.